# Design Thinking
## *in the Classroom*

# Design Thinking

## *in the Classroom*

Easy-to-Use Teaching Tools
to Foster Creativity, Encourage Innovation
and Unleash Potential in Every Student

## David Lee

 Ulysses Press

Published in the United States by:
Ulysses Press
P.O. Box 3440
Berkeley, CA 94703
www.ulyssespress.com

ISBN: 978-1-61243-801-6
Library of Congress Control Number 2018930779

Printed in the United States by Kingery Printing Company
10 9 8 7 6 5 4 3 2 1

Acquisitions editor: Bridget Thoreson
Managing editor: Claire Chun
Editor: Renee Rutledge
Proofreader: Lauren Harrison
Index: Sayre Van Young
Front cover design: Justin Shirley
Interior design and layout: what!design @ whatweb.com
Cover art: © Tancha/shutterstock.com

Distributed by Publishers Group West

To Landon, my joy and motivation;
Angela, my love and best friend;
and Christine, the most courageous person I know

# Contents

*Part Two*

## The Design Thinking Process 45

*Chapter Three*

*Chapter Four*

*Chapter Five*

*Part Three*

# Design Thinking in the Classroom     155

*Preface*

# Driven By My Past

I don't like to reminisce about my schooling years. When I reflect on my past experiences, I end up getting agitated and start to think about what could've been, how I felt unable to reach my full potential. Growing up I was a shy student who never wanted to share my opinions or ideas because I thought they were not valuable. I didn't have the confidence in my ability to solve problems or create solutions to produce great work. These experiences led me to believe that only "special" people were capable of being successful—people who were innately creative and natural problem-solvers. I continuously overheard teachers tell specific students that they were "naturals," making it seem like their high-performing abilities were genetic. Even when learning about successful Americans like Thomas Edison, George Washington, and Martin Luther King, Jr., the stories of their failures were rarely discussed, and if they were, it was with very little thought. I came to believe that to be successful I had to have the traits that these famous people seemed to innately possess: a brilliant mind, competitiveness, confidence, assertiveness, and ingenuity. At an early age, I believed I had none of these traits.

As I got older, I slowly realized that this belief was not true. I found that everyone already had these traits, including me, but they were not being developed to their fullest potential. These traits needed to be rigorously applied through continuous practice and training. Gradually unlearning the fear of failure that had been instilled in me through my education, I stopped looking for the one right answer when approaching problems. Everyone is creative and a potential change-maker—we just have to practice! I soon realized I wanted to show young people that they have the qualities needed to be successful and capable of improving themselves and the world around them. That was when I decided to become an educator. From that moment, my purpose in life was to empower every student I taught, to develop systems and habits of learning that render them future-ready citizens who have the skills, dispositions, and learning abilities to succeed in their endeavors.

Next, I needed to figure out how I was going to empower my students. What skills and tools would I need to teach them? The answer arrived in April of 2014 when I attended an informal conference called Beyond Laptops at Yokohama International School in Yokohama, Japan. This conference provides attendees the opportunity to take a deep dive into educational issues through collaborative discussions, hands-on activities, and reflections. One component of the conference focuses on the future and how education can better prepare students for what lies ahead by identifying essential skills. In this particular year, a whole day was dedicated to the design thinking approach and how it could transform education. In a session led by technology integrationists Heather Dowd and Patrick Green, we quickly experienced the design thinking process, got a sense of the goals in design thinking, and learned how each phase gets you to a solution. In one hour, I was able to identify and define a problem for a teacher, brainstorm wild ideas, and prototype a solution that could be used to resolve this problem.

That day helped me to see the potential of design thinking and how it could help me accomplish my vision to develop empowered, creative problem-solvers. By adopting this design approach, students have the opportunity to think critically and imaginatively, collaborate, communicate, tackle setbacks, and engage their curiosity. They can develop into autonomous learners who decide how they work and what solutions they want to create. Most importantly, design thinking provides a structured scaffold and a set of mindsets that allow students to effectively approach any type of problem or project with courage and confidence.

I envisioned this solution-based methodology transforming students into innovators and potentially transforming the way I teach. It would require me to design authentic learning experiences that simulate what goes on in the real world, providing opportunities for students to engage in inquiry and gain critical knowledge and skills from multiple disciplines to solve meaningful problems.

My hope in this book is to give you a better understanding of the benefits of design thinking for students. I will provide strategies on how to effectively teach the different learning practices of the process and culture, share valuable information on how to develop authentic projects that incorporate design thinking meaningfully, and summarize a number of engaging projects.

# *Part 1*

# What Is Design Thinking?

# Challenges of a Rapidly Changing Workplace

We are living in a world of rapid change where new problems are arising, such as overpopulation, lack of natural resources, and cyber threats, and it is becoming difficult to predict the problems that our students will face in the future. Due to these rapid changes, the way we work is being redefined, moving away from routine tasks to nonroutine work. According to David H. Autor, an economics professor at MIT, **routine tasks** are characterized as "middle-skilled cognitive and production activities, such as bookkeeping, clerical work, and repetitive production tasks" that require workers to follow "precise, well-understood procedures." In contrast, **nonroutine tasks** are abstract activities that require "problem-solving, intuition, persuasion, and creativity" and involve analytic skills such as interpersonal skills. Additionally, nonroutine tasks can involve manual work that requires "situational adaptability" and "in-person interaction."

In his research, Autor found that routine tasks in the US workplace have slowly decreased in the last 50 years, while nonroutine tasks that require analytical, interpersonal, and adaptive skills have increased. Research by the World Bank has shown that jobs in 30 other countries increasingly require nonroutine skills as well. For this reason, educators will need to provide students with learning experiences that require nonroutine tasks.

The change in job makeup may be connected to the current and competitive knowledge economy, described by Tony Wagner's *The Global Achievement Gap* as an economy that consists of jobs "that can be broken down into a routine, transformed into bits and bytes, and exported to other countries where there is a rapidly increasing number of highly educated 'knowledge workers' who will work for a small fraction of the salary of a comparable American worker." Wagner, an Expert in Residence at Harvard University's new Innovation Lab, states that the knowledge economy challenges workers with an overwhelming abundance of information, continuously changing technologies, and the emergence of more complex challenges. This brings up a couple of questions: How will our students gain success in this type of economy? And how are we going to help our students differentiate themselves from the competition due to globalization?

One approach to this problem is for teachers to teach and model the design thinking (DT) method. This method provides students with the opportunity to develop a creative process called the Seven Survival Skills, discussed in the following pages, as well as cultivate mindsets and dispositions that are crucial to success as workers, citizens, and lifelong learners. It is our responsibility as educators to focus on preparing students to function successfully. Incorporating design thinking into your classroom will help them approach problems and tasks in an innovative and effective manner that can be valuable for any future endeavor.

# Seven Survival Skills

Wagner decided to ask a variety of leaders from multiple fields what qualities they look for in employees of today's workplace. After talking to leaders from business, nonprofit, philanthropic, and educational organizations, he identified Seven Survival Skills that are essential for the twenty-first century:

**1. Critical thinking and problem-solving:** Ability to sift through information, gain a deep understanding of a problem and its context, and apply relevant information to find solutions through a spirit of inquiry.

**2. Collaboration across networks and learning by influence:** Ability to learn from and work with groups from diverse cultures harmoniously, and influence others through persuasion and reasoning within a trusting relationship.

**3. Agility and adaptability:** Ability to maneuver through distractions and obstacles, to make appropriate changes to better suit a workplace of continuous change, or to pivot an objective because of a new need discovered through copious amounts of information or the emergence of complex problems.

**4. Initiative and entrepreneurialism:** Ability to take self-directed actions and seek new opportunities to bring change, make improvements, and find solutions to difficult problems.

**5. Effective oral and written communication:** Ability to clearly and effectively share ideas and thoughts to others from different perspectives and cultures.

**6. Assessing and analyzing information:** Ability to sift through and evaluate an immense quantity of readily available information to identify valuable knowledge that can lead to solutions.

**7. Curiosity and imagination:** Eagerness to learn about the ambiguous and interesting, and to think about what can be improved or reinvented through the use of creativity.

# Successful Teachers in Innovation

As I read about these survival skills, I couldn't help but think about the educators I've worked with who exhibited these particular skills and were able to thrive, even when their school was moving away from traditional approaches and implementing innovative initiatives and practices. In 2015, a school in Korea asked me to implement a STEM initiative called the KoLAB Program. The "Ko" stood for Korea, "LAB" for the learning spaces we used for STEM work, and "KoLAB" for collaboration. Our goal was to give every student an authentic learning experience where they rigorously applied knowledge and skills from multiple disciplines to solve meaningful problems and answer real-world questions.

The KoLAB Program drastically transformed the way education was being delivered and received, enabling students and teachers to become risk-takers and innovators. It combined transdisciplinary STEM education, project-based learning, design thinking, and the maker movement into one learning experience. Due to these drastic changes, implementing the program was very difficult; it required mindsets and teaching approaches that many of the teachers were unfamiliar with. A few teachers struggled with the new educational approach; however, many others thrived. The teachers who were successful had most or all of the Seven Survival Skills.

For instance, one successful teacher in the KoLAB program, Elizabeth DiRenzo, was able to use rational thinking skills to evaluate the quality of a particular aspect of the program, and developed new solutions to issues, improving upon what already existed (critical thinking and problem-solving). DiRenzo helped strengthen the connection between subject areas in transdisciplinary projects, provided strategies in improving unit maps, developed standards-based assessments that tracked students' mastery, and implemented student reflections into every unit to help them consider the significance of what they learned.

Many problems that we faced in the program were not anticipated, so teachers like DiRenzo needed to think quickly to understand new challenges that arose, making the appropriate modifications to the way they thought, acted, or taught to resolve these challenges (agility and adaptability). Oftentimes, self-directed teachers approached me with new strategies, tools, or solutions that would improve the quality of the program, and took the lead in implementing a new initiative (initiative and entrepreneurialism). For example, DiRenzo found a need for students to track their progress and growth, especially when using the scientific method and the DT process. She decided to start experimenting with Seesaw, a digital portfolio platform. Our team soon adopted the platform, and many others at the school quickly followed suit. Instead of asking me what to do in a situation, she was able to identify the problem, think on her feet, and then react decisively to the situation.

Our teachers worked extensively together to develop and improve transdisciplinary units that integrated knowledge and skills from multiple subject areas into one common project. This required homeroom teachers and specialists in science, design, technology, etc., to collaborate in developing engaging standards-based units, as well as making sure that all the lessons in each subject area were aligned with one another (collaboration across networks and learning by influence). Inquisitive teachers provided creative ideas for meaningful, authentic learning (curiosity and imagination) and were able to persuade others of their ideas through clear and concise communication (effective oral and written communication). Finally, a successful KoLAB teacher was able to sift through and evaluate numerous educational resources, identifying the most effective ones that could be used to improve the program (assessing and analyzing information).

# Interview with a CEO

Fascinated by Wagner's findings, I decided to do my own research by interviewing a company leader to find out what skills he or she was looking for in an employee, the skills that would help a person thrive and contribute greatly to an organization. During back-to-school night, I was fortunate enough to chat with David Y. Lee, a father of one of my students and also the CEO of Shakr. Shakr is a digital platform that allows small businesses to easily create professional videos. It currently has $13 million in venture capital funding. Lee graciously obliged my request to interview him for this book.

David said he hires the following type of people for his company:

*"People who don't wait. I have zero qualms about someone leaving our company who needs to be told what to do. If I have to think about what to tell this person to do, then there is a problem. I think that the best performers have been the ones who take cues or the specific instructions, either way, and act to create their own work. I'm a pretty imaginative person, but I find my imagination is grossly inadequate for what I intend to do in this world. I think my imagination needs to be supplemented by the imaginations around me. To a certain extent we need to be synced, but then they [need to] go on a tangent and go a lot deeper, far deeper than I could because I think my job is to set a general direction of the company."*

To illustrate his point, David described his current Director of Video Effectiveness at Shakr. While she was an intern in her third year of university, David mentioned to her that he was thinking about creating a revenue share program so that designers outside of the company would have an incentive to build video templates for Shakr. However, some of the designers in Shakr were concerned. Without any prompting, she created a website that explained the third-party program and wrote up all the documents and legal agreements. Her initiative, entrepreneurialism, and communication skills convinced the Shakr designers of the incredible benefits the program would have for the company, and in a span of a year, the company's third-party contracts grew from only two to a thousand. Even though she was not trained in doing any of these tasks, she was able to proactively create something tangible from what David imagined, immediately transforming the landscape of the business in a drastic way.

David believes that schools also need to provide students with the opportunity to work on creative pursuits that are more centered around problem-solving to develop the next generation of workers and creators. "I remember growing up having teachers telling me that 'That's just the way it is,'" he says. "There should be no child anywhere whose curiosity is limited by society's ability to feed that curiosity." With students being naturally curious and motivated intrinsically to seek out knowledge, David adds that there is little that can stand in our way other than active discouragement, and there is so much of this. To him, it's the role of parents, teachers, and schools to feed the curiosity of students and remove as many active discouragements in their learning and pursuits as possible.

# A Challenge for Today's Teachers

If these skills are what is required to be successful in our students' future workplace, then why aren't schools preparing them with these survival skills? One reason is the current standardized testing system where teachers and schools are accountable for what their students should know.

Since student performance on these tests are tied to funding for the school and the employment of teachers, many schools and teachers have made preparation for these tests their number one priority, resulting in curriculum consisting of test prep. If these tests, most often in the form of multiple choice, don't require students to think critically, problem-solve, communicate effectively, or analyze information, then why would teachers use their valuable instructional time to focus on these skills?

Another reason for the lack is that many educators teach the way they were taught, which mostly took place in a traditional education setting, where a teacher stood in front of the class providing the information students needed to know. Students would be required to memorize the information and then regurgitate it back to the teacher in some form. Few projects required problem-solving, critical thinking, and creativity. I believe many teachers continue to teach this way because it's the safest method, and, for them, the most comfortable way for students to learn. However, this approach doesn't prepare students with the learning tools that are required in their future endeavors outside of the education space. Their careers and daily lives will require learning that doesn't involve rote memorization and regurgitating information, but assessing and analyzing information, communication, collaboration, and ongoing, self-guided inquiry.

Schools and teachers should be developing curriculum that provides students with authentic educational experiences where they are collaborating with others, using their curiosity and imagination, and demonstrating initiative and entrepreneurship to create high-quality work. Implementing design thinking into this authentic educational setting ignites students to grapple with complex challenges, develop their Seven Survival Skills, and gain the ability to apply creative problem-solving practices. Equipping students with the toolkit of design thinking can prepare them for a world that is becoming more uncertain and ambiguous, and help them effectively approach problems in an innovative and efficacious manner that can be valuable for most future endeavors.

*Chapter One*

# Design Thinking and Why It Matters

In a world of constant change and innovation, we need to change the education we provide our students, focusing less on *what* students should learn and more on *how* they should learn. As discussed, it is crucial for us as educators to foster and exemplify learning behaviors and dispositions that will help them solve ambiguous, complex problems and succeed in their future endeavors. This can be realized through the implementation of design thinking in the classroom. DT will allow your students to approach any type of problem or circumstance like a designer, becoming agents of change for their community and the world.

Design thinking is a human-centered methodology that democratizes the design process by providing the structure and tools for every person to think and behave like a designer. In our context, we will define a *designer* as a person who uses the design process and strategies to think, plan, and take action in improving a situation/experience or solving a particular problem. The DT process consists of five phases: empathize, define, ideate, prototype, and test. Each of these phases has a particular goal, with actions that help designers achieve this goal. We will delve more into each phase in Chapter 3, The Five Phases of Design Thinking.

This process all starts with empathy work, where designers gain a deep understanding of their end users, the group of people who will benefit from their work. Designers must learn about end user needs to design an impactful solution to a problem or improve an end user experience.

Most people understand design thinking as a process; however, it is much more than that. To properly utilize the process, designers need to understand the philosophy behind the approach and possess essential attitudes and mindsets that make them prone to innovative behaviors and actions. We will dive deeper into its mindsets in Chapter 2, More Than a Process: DT Mindsets.

Design thinking is a difficult concept to define because it encompasses so many ideas and beliefs. It is also a concept that is being implemented in multiple fields, giving rise to new definitions and uses. For our purposes, we keep design thinking in the context of education and our students. But before we do this, let's dive into how the term "design thinking" gained its popularity.

# Design and Business

Tim Brown, the CEO and president of IDEO, a design and innovation company that popularized design thinking, defines the methodology for the business world as a "human-centered approach to innovation that draws from the designer's toolkit to integrate the needs of people, the possibilities of technology, and the requirements for business success." In his book, *Change By Design*, he gives a more universal definition that is suitable for multiple fields and situations, adding that the design thinking approach generates "new ideas that tackle the global challenges of health, poverty, and education; new strategies that result in differences that matter and a sense of purpose that engages everyone affected by them." Gradually, IDEO and other organizations started to transition from designing tangible products to designing and improving real-world experiences.

Since 1991, IDEO has designed solutions to problems in branding, energy, education, the environment, experience design, financial services, and many other fields. One of IDEO's earliest designs was the first mouse for Apple. Steve Jobs challenged the company and its founder, David Kelley, to design an intuitive mouse for every Apple computer for only 17 dollars. Since then, they have helped design kidney transporters for transplants that doubled storage time, spinal-surgery instruments that improve accuracy during procedures, a new modular voting system for Los Angeles County that is intuitive, accessible, and adaptable over time, and an interactive learning experience for kids to learn coding called Project Bloks, just to name a few.

These solutions were designed through a combination of human-centered design and a culture of innovation that was coined "design thinking" on account of Kelley frequently using the word "thinking" to describe what he did as a designer. Design thinking flourished in the business world because it allowed companies to react to changing trends, empathize with consumer needs, and not function solely on analytical thinking.

Today a number of companies have transformed their business models through the implementation of design thinking to stay relevant and innovate in a world of rapidly changing trends. The South Korean technology giant Samsung has incorporated key design thinking concepts into its company's structure and policies, learning to integrate empathy and experimentation into its "risk-averse culture." The company also established its own in-house design group, the Corporate Design Center, that focuses on using design thinking to plan for Samsung's future. This pushed Samsung from a manufacturing company that produced inexpensive, imitative electronics to one that produces new and innovative products.

IBM, a computer hardware and software corporation that offers hosting and consulting services, has changed its focus from engineering to user needs and experience. In 2012, there was one designer in the company for every 80 computer programmers. In 2016 the number of designers grew, with one designer for every 20 programmers. IBM has developed its own version of the design thinking process that they feel could help big corporations remain relevant in an innovation economy.

My favorite example of a business using design thinking is GE Healthcare, a company that provides medical technologies and services. Innovation architect Doug Dietz had been working on a specific MRI scanner for two years and was excited to get an opportunity to see it installed in a hospital. However, what he observed gave him a new perspective on his work and reframed his problem to focus on the user.

In his TEDx Talk, "Transforming Healthcare for Children and Their Families," Dietz describes two parents walking toward the MRI room with their seven-year-old daughter, who was upset and filled with anxiety due to the upcoming procedure. According to Dietz, the dark MRI room consisted of a warning sticker with an exclamation point, yellow and black caution tape on the floor, and the MRI machine that made a terrible noise and "looked like a brick with a hole in it." Seeing the little girl's terrified reaction to his scanner, he realized that he needed to focus on making the stressful experience more pleasant and fun for his users. He gained empathy with children by visiting a local daycare and talking to pediatric health care professionals to find out what children went through as patients. He collaborated with a team of educators from a local children's museum and a group of medical professionals to produce ideas that could help make the scanning experience enjoyable.

Using his new understandings, Dietz designed the GE Adventure Series, themed scanning experiences that made medical procedures more like exciting adventures. For example, the Pirate Adventure transformed the medical setting into the dock of a pirate ship, where the patients are scanned on its plank. In the Coral City Adventure, patients in the emergency room go into a yellow submarine for their procedures, with the sound of harps in the background. In the Cozy Camp, patients are placed in a camping scene where they are scanned in a sleeping bag under the starry night. With these new magical settings and experiences, satisfaction scores from children rose up to 90 percent, with some children asking parents if they could do the procedure again, demonstrating the power of empathy on insightful design. These companies are now being recognized by their customers because they are designing based on customer needs instead of gaining attention through advertisements.

# Design Thinking for Education

Tim Brown's definition of DT is great for the business world, but what about a definition in the context of education, especially in terms of students using the methodology? Using my experience in teaching DT in the classroom, I have formulated the following definition:

Design thinking is a combination of human-centered, inquiry-based scaffolding and innovation-friendly mindsets where students apply transdisciplinary knowledge/skills with creative practices to collaboratively discover empathetic insights, generate and explore radical ideas, and create, test, and improve tangible outcomes; it is having courage and attempting to bring meaningful change to people's (or their own) lives, improve real-world experiences, or develop solutions to complex problems.

## Why It Matters

As stated earlier, DT is crucial for students to develop into future-ready citizens who can learn and have the confidence to tackle challenges no matter the situation or circumstance, who are able to learn continuously in a world of constant change and innovation. DT is also a great method for students to use in highly effective educational approaches such as project-based learning (PBL) and in science, technology, engineering, and mathematics (STEM) education. PBL is a teaching approach that consists of students working on an extended project to address a meaningful problem or question that is embedded in real-world context. According to Jo Anne Vasquez, a PhD STEM consultant, STEM education is "an interdisciplinary approach to learning that removes traditional barriers separating the four disciplines of science, technology, engineering, and mathematics, and integrates them into real-world, rigorous, and relevant learning experiences for students."

Both the PBL and STEM approaches focus on real-world experiences and require sustained inquiry where teachers take on the role of facilitators, spark the curiosity of students, and guide their students' learning. Instead of a learning environment where students are given facts, students continually ask questions to gain a deep understanding of a problem and investigate further to produce a solution. What better method to use than DT, where students operate through the five phases to arrive at innovative solutions, developing into autonomous learners who are responsible for their own learning? DT provides students the vehicle for inquiry, teaching them how to think, reason, analyze, empathize, and use their natural curiosity to find solutions in these transformative education approaches.

DT also provides opportunities for best practices to occur in teaching and learning. For example, in a third-grade project, students were tasked to program a virtual wildlife sanctuary that would help protect and increase the population of an endangered species through captive breeding. In social studies, students explored the idea of government meeting the needs and demands of citizens with laws and policies that create new responsibilities, protect freedoms, and create positive change. They took on the role of lobbyists who sought to persuade members of the government to create policies to fund the creation of a wildlife sanctuary for a specific endangered species. Using the DT method and what they learned in science, they developed a blueprint for a sanctuary that was appropriate for their species' life cycle.

Additionally, students used what they learned about inherited traits and the variation of traits among individuals of the same species to "design" an ideal offspring through theoretical selective breeding. Since third graders knew that some traits gave individuals an advantage in surviving, finding mates, and reproducing, they identified which females and males would be selected for breeding to produce healthy, strong, and advantageous offspring in their virtual wildlife sanctuary.

In technology, students learned basic programming concepts to create their virtual wildlife sanctuary, which they published online to share with the public.

In my experience, students who use the DT method are more engaged because of their challenging and interesting topics. The third graders were intrigued by and learned the relevance of what they were learning. DT projects also support a climate of inquiry where students are responsible for their own learning, going through the different phases of the process to pose questions, investigate, and apply the knowledge and skills they gain to meaningful challenges. It also increases the opportunity for collaboration and provides multiple instances for meaningful feedback from the teacher and peers.

Additionally, DT can help students see problems and challenges in a positive light as opportunities for improvement, change, and resolution. It empowers them with the skills and confidence to believe they could make a constructive impact on any situation, even if they are not an expert in the issue. They'll believe they have the capacity to be creative designers who can come up with new and effective ideas. DT gives them the permission to fail, learn from their failures, and improve upon their solutions with an optimistic and enthusiastic attitude.

Imagine if students learned the DT process starting in kindergarten. What complex problems would they be able to solve by the time they got to high school? What new problems would they be able to identify that we were unaware of? Imagine them leaving our schools for the real world with the belief that they have the power to make positive, impactful change for people around the world and the confidence to pursue and embark on projects that they would have never dreamed of working on. Imagine them being aware of the infinite possibilities of what they can do and who they can be. This confidence is best described by David Wallace, an engineering professor at MIT, who said, "More than anything I hope they [students] have the confidence and perhaps a little bit of arrogance to think that they can solve just about any problem, but at the same time be humble enough that they realize they're going to have to work really hard to get there." Like Wallace, I believe equipping students with DT skills and mindsets will help them gain the confidence to solve any problem they face.

During the first year of implementing DT into our elementary school, a fourth-grade student approached me in the hallway. He was a new student who was uncertain in his abilities, found it challenging to complete simple tasks on his own, and was always scared to try new things because of his fear of failure. I was just like him as a fourth grader. I know what it's like to be afraid, withdrawn, insecure, and timid. To my surprise and excitement, he told me, "Mr. Lee, I feel really confident, like I can accomplish anything." DT has been able to empower him and unlock his human creative potential.

*Chapter Two*

# More Than a Process: DT Mindsets

After learning about DT at the conference workshop, I immediately went home and devised a plan to have students use the process for a project. At the time, DT was only a process to me, a magical step-by-step method that had the potential to transform "unimaginative" students into wondrous creatives. I quickly realized the process itself wasn't magical. It gave them strategies to think creatively, but the products they produced weren't particularly inventive or innovative; no one seemed to be going beyond the obvious. This went on for the first year until I realized that DT is not only a process, but a specific way of thinking (hence its name, design *thinking*). The values and mindset allow creative outcomes to emerge. In this sense I believe the culture of DT is much more valuable than the actual process.

In his webinar, *Design Thinking = Method, Not Magic*, Bill Burnett, the Executive Director of Stanford's Product Design program, talked about the phrase, "Culture eats strategy for breakfast." Originally developed by Peter Drucker, an American management consultant, the phrase describes how it is ineffectual to use a process that is not compatible with the culture of a group. It is the group's culture that affects how people work, behave, and make decisions. Burnett explained, "If you have the wrong kind of culture it doesn't matter what process you use…it won't make any difference because culture rejects the process. Culture is always stronger than the process or programs that people put in place because culture is the unspoken rules of behavior of any organization, and that's how, really, things get done."

I observed this firsthand when my students attempted to solve problems using the DT process. Their behaviors, actions, and interactions with one another were not conducive to producing desired results with the DT process. They had difficulty designing a solution based on end user preferences and needs rather than their own. They were fearful to try new things, make mistakes, and fail in their work, which many times led to doubt, pessimism, and a tendency to give up. Some believed that they held fixed traits in "lower" intelligence and talent that correlated to lower work performance. I've realized that my students were not able to effectively use the DT process because they did not share core values that encompass a culture of innovation, which makes the effective execution of DT possible. In this chapter we will identify the mindsets and beliefs that can foster an efficacious and authentic use of DT in the classroom.

# Six Key Mindsets

A mindset is a set of attitudes that reflect how a person thinks or feels about a particular thing. These attitudes can affect the way they behave in a particular scenario. For example, if a student has a fear of failure and never wants to make mistakes, then he or she would be likely to hesitate in taking action, making important decisions, and trying new things when working in the DT process.

Founded by David Kelley, the d.school, Stanford's design institute, provides students with learning experiences that "unlock their creative potential" through the application of DT in multidisciplinary, real-world challenges. The d.school has created a program called the K12 Lab Network that promotes the implementation of DT into classrooms and schools to bring capacity and agency to educators who want to create positive change in education.

According to the K12 Lab Network wiki, six key mindsets are required by designers to use DT to its fullest potential:

**1.** Human centered

**2.** Mindful of process

**3.** Culture of prototyping

**4.** Bias toward action

**5.** Show don't tell

**6.** Radical collaboration

These mindsets help students behave and perform like design thinkers who produce novel solutions to problems and challenges, and ingrain a self-belief that they can take action to bring positive change. The six key mindsets have been defined through actionable, "Students will be able to…" statements based on the work of the K12 Lab Network.

## Human Centered

*Students will be able to gain inspiration and direction from users and respond to human needs by placing the user at the center of all empathy work.*

Students who have a human-centered mindset are able to think in the perspective of others, particularly the person/people they are designing a solution for. They can "walk in the person's shoes" to gain an understanding of their needs and wants. The prevailing focus throughout the DT process and in each phase are the people we are designing for. They are the most important factors in the design process. Engaging and interacting with these people can result in the emergence of inspirations and insights that direct designs to desired outcomes. We will discuss more about the human-centered mindset and how empathy techniques can help students develop this mindset, and will review some examples of human-centered learning experiences in the following chapter.

## Mindful of Process

*Students will be able to be thoughtful and reflective of the work being done, how the work is being done, and how the work will improve.*

The mindful-of-process mindset enables students to think about the work they are doing in a particular phase of the design process. Each phase has its own purpose, goals, and strategies. For example, if a student is in the ideate phase, where they are collaboratively brainstorming a solution for a particular problem, they will need to be open-minded, defer judgment, think beyond the obvious, build on the ideas of others, and generate a large volume of ideas. Being attentive to these behaviors, goals, and thinking will allow students to be get the most out of each phase in the DT process. A crucial part of this mindset is reflecting on how the work is being done and how it can be improved in each phase.

## Culture of Prototyping

*Students will be able to explore and experiment, build things to learn and think things through, and engage users with prototypes to elicit and receive feedback.*

With this mindset, the process of creating artifacts or solutions allows students to continuously learn and apply their new learnings to improve what they've built or developed; ultimately, this will result in high-quality products or solutions. This build-to-think mentality is best described by David Kelley: "This building, this doing, prototyping, whatever we're going to call it, is a way of thinking as opposed to the kind of grubby thing manufacturing does after all the decisions are made. We spend a lot of time getting the students [...] to kind of think about how can you be really clever about jumping right in and finding out as much as you can from building."

A student with a prototyping mindset is inclined to rapidly create and test to quickly learn from failures and receive feedback. They use their creativity to apply what they have learned to make improvements to their artifacts or solutions. This iterative, trial-and-error process of prototyping is done so frequently that it results in desired outcomes in a shorter period of time.

## Bias Toward Action

*Students will be action-oriented to quickly think and learn, as well as make decisions.*

A bias-toward-action mindset gives students the tendency to take initiative, make decisions, and take self-directed actions. This mindset is extremely important to DT because all the phases in the process require students to have action-oriented behavior. For example, in the empathize phase, students need to engage with people and experience their perspective to gain a deep understanding of the challenges they face. In the test phase, students need to perform repeated tests to gain valuable data and feedback that is later synthesized and used to make improvements.

To have a bias toward action, students need to overcome their fear of failure so that they don't simply try and give up when obstacles arise. Fear and self-doubt can debilitate students from taking risks or acting upon a spark or revelation. Overcoming this fear and embracing failure allows students to be creative, generate a wide range of ideas and possibilities, and try out novel and audacious things. Action-oriented behavior occurs when students realize that failure is not the outcome but part of the process, and with an ample amount of iterations, their prototype will transform into a high-quality product or solution.

## Show Don't Tell

*Students will be able to communicate and share ideas visually for clarity, understanding, and decision-making.*

With the show-don't-tell mindset, students communicate and share ideas through visual representations in the form of a sketch, tangible prototype, or digital visualizations. These visuals can make a complex idea easier to understand and bring clarity to information that might be perplexing. A simple sketch can stimulate further discussions, identify unanticipated problems, and bring everyone on your team on the same page. Showing your ideas can also help organize your thoughts and improve the information you want to communicate clearly. Since sharing visual ideas is a great opportunity for gaining feedback from stakeholders, it is important for students to be open-minded to constructive criticism and refrain from defensiveness so that they can learn and their ideas can improve.

## Radical Collaboration

*Students will be able to collaborate and create partnerships with people of different disciplines as well as the users to develop innovative ideas and solutions.*

Students who have a radical-collaboration mindset are able to learn and work together effectively using social and interpersonal skills to complete a common goal. A team's diverse set of perspectives, skills, backgrounds, and learning styles leads to a wide range of possibilities, breakthrough ideas, and innovative solutions. What makes this mindset radical are the collaborative opportunities with stakeholders outside of the design team. For example, designers can collaborate with the people they are designing for, creating an inclusive partnership where the end user is seen as a viable expert. Additionally, since DT is used for real-world challenges and problems, it is important for students to work with experts from multiple disciplines. In the school setting, students would collaborate with teachers who are experts in a particular field.

This mindset values teamwork—students and teachers working together effectively and efficiently for one common goal. Teamwork takes place in a family-like atmosphere where students build positive relationships based on trust and appreciation of one another. In caring for their teammates, they also apply empathy with the emotions and feelings. Valuing teamwork minimizes the occurrence of hierarchical relationships where a few individuals assert dominance in a project. Minimizing competition between students also helps increase morale, improve relationships, and reduce discouragement.

# Other Mindsets for Success

## Improve/Learn from Failures

As stated earlier, it is important for students to overcome their fear of failure so that they can have a bias-toward-action mindset. Students must also understand that failure is essential to learning and improving whatever is being designed. They must change the way they view failure and see it as a way to identify what needs to be improved. "Don't think of it as failure," explains Tim Brown. "Think of it as designing experiments through which you're going to learn." It is a mindset that pushes a person to strive for continual improvement in their work.

When my students first used the DT process, they were scared to test out their prototypes because of their fear of failure. They were worried about how their peers would view them if they failed, and how their failed tests would reveal evidence of their "inadequate" abilities, intelligence, and/or ideas. As they completed more DT projects, they realized that they were constantly jumping back and forth from prototyping to testing, identifying failure points in their design, making appropriate improvements, and finally, going back to testing their prototypes. With this iterative process and a learning environment that gave them the permission to fail, my students soon developed a strong mindset of embracing failure as a powerful tool to learn about new insights and make improvements on their designs, with some students completely unperturbed by the notion of failure.

## Creative Confidence

According to David Kelley, creative confidence is believing one has the ability to come up with new ideas and the courage to try them out. This mindset stems from the idea that everyone holds the "creative trait," but like a muscle, it is a trait that needs to be exercised and strengthened. The idea that everyone holds this creative trait is most apparent when teaching junior kindergarten and kindergarten students. When they brainstorm ideas for solutions to a problem, they think of the most imaginative and inventive ideas.

However, this unfiltered thinking and willingness to try new things seems to decrease when working with older students. When working with upper-elementary students, we spend more of my time developing their creative confidence, slowly chipping away their firm belief that only those who are innately born with the trait have the potential to be truly creative. Gradually, students develop a confidence in their ability to be creative and apply their creativity into real-world work through the use of specific strategies and practices, and by working in a learning environment that nurtures creative work.

## Creative "Courage"

David Clifford from K12 Lab and Design School X uses the term
"courage" instead of "confidence." This phrasing reflects how we,
as design thinkers, are learning to or have the ability to overcome
our fear of creatively tackling daunting challenges. We are constantly
overcoming our fear of failure or being stuck when generating
new ideas. The phrase "creative courage" is especially suitable for
students who are learning to be creative through the use of the DT
process and their development of DT mindsets. As educators, our
goal is for our students to eventually manifest creative confidence, a
self-assurance in their ability to be creative, but it is important to let
them know that this end result starts with courage.

# Growth Mindset

In her book *Mindset: The New Psychology of Success*, Carol Dweck identifies
two mindsets that she discovered when researching which types of people
succeed. She found that some people have either a fixed mindset, the belief
that an individual is born with a fixed degree of ability and intelligence,
or a growth mindset, the belief that a person can increase their ability and
intelligence through deliberate practice, significant energy, and relentless
persistence. The latter mindset is essential for students when using the
DT process because it gives them practical optimism.

Through continuous learning, practice, and dedication, students gain a
hopeful confidence about bringing a positive effect to any given situation
through their attitude and actions. They understand that obstacles are
not permanent barriers that impede them from their goals, but temporary setbacks that can be overcome through effective learning practices.
Students with a growth mindset ignore their initial reaction to hesitate
when confronted with a problem, believe that it's possible to solve complex
problems, and ultimately, feel like they can accomplish a goal no matter
the circumstance or degree of complexity.

# Beginner's Mindset

It is important for students to gain a beginner's mindset when empathizing with users. A beginner's mindset is a concept from Zen Buddhism that involves the attitude of thinking and seeing from a novice's point of view. This attitude helps students become more eager to learn about a topic and be open to the things that they learn. Thinking like a learner instead of an expert allows them to grow and improve with humility, but most importantly, it deters closed-mindedness that can hinder their ability to obtain insights that can spark inspiration. As stated earlier, design thinkers are not always experts in the topic they are designing for, but instead are experts in the design process. Empathy cannot truly be attained when students think they already know enough about a topic. Their presumptions could be misunderstandings that can hinder empathy work, restricting the possibilities to gain meaningful insights that lead to truly creative ideas.

There are a few principles students should follow (and teachers should promote) to obtain a beginner's mindset when engaging in empathy work. According to the d.school, it is important for design thinkers to not judge or advance their own opinions on what they observe or learn during empathy work. This requires students to be aware of—and put aside—their biases and assumptions so that they can genuinely empathize with others.

Students need to also respectfully listen with great intent to what end users and experts in the topic have to say. Listening should be a conscious, active effort to understand what is being said and how it's being said, and to actually feel what the speaker is feeling. Listening is done without interrupting the speaker, imposing an agenda onto the conversation, or engaging the natural impulse to form counter talking points while the other person is talking. Instead, students should wait for the speaker to finish their answer or thought before being asked further clarifying questions.

This leads to the next principle of a beginner's mindset, "question every-thing." Students should question as much as they can to acquire a deeper understanding of the end user and the context of the design challenge. This can be done by asking the follow-up question of "why" or "how" to uncover hidden stories, emotions, and other insights. Also, asking good questions about everything will allow students to gain information about their end user's needs and perspective that can help solve their problems.

To ask good questions, students must truly be curious and see the world through a beginner's eyes of wonderment. The majority of us would be intrigued when learning about rocket science that enables people to live on other planets, since it is a field that we are unfamiliar with. In empa-thy work, students need to assume the same type of curiosity even if a topic seems mundane or familiar. In *Creative Confidence*, David Kelley states that we need to see the world and think the way we would when we travel to a foreign city. He stated, "On a trip, we become our own version of Sherlock Holmes, intensely observing the environment around us. Continuously trying to figure out a world that is foreign and new. Too often, we go through day-to-day life on cruise control, oblivious to huge swaths of our surroundings." Being curious can be driven by the urge to find an unexpected or surprising insight. In the classroom, I overhear students expressing excitement when they learn about a surprising fact that could influence their design. Teach your students that their curiosity is a valuable asset when it comes to DT.

## Liberatory Design Mindsets

Liberatory Design is an adaptation of Stanford d.school's DT process that includes two additional phases, Notice and Reflect. Developed in partnership with the K12 Lab Network and the National Equity Project, the Liberatory Design process ensures that designers focus on equity and inclusion in their designs. In the Notice phase, prior to empathizing with the context of the design challenge and the end users, designers work to build a self-awareness of their own identity, biases, emotions, and assumptions. Noticing their authentic self allows designers to empathize with a beginner's mindset to develop equity-centered design. In the Reflect phase, students learn to focus on their actions, emotions, insights, and impact within the user's context to see what changes can be made to increase equity, inclusiveness, and aesthetics.

With these new adaptations come a new adaptation of the DT mindsets. The Liberatory Design mindsets are more complex and would be suitable for educators who teach design thinking to grade 6 to 12 students, as well as educators who want to design equitable learning environments. The following are the mindsets required for designers to use the Liberatory Design process effectively. The mindsets are expressed as actionable statements.

- **Practice self-awareness** to minimize harmful effects of privilege and oppression to the design process.

- **Focus on human values** to place the users at the center of all empathy work.

- **Recognize oppression** to identify inequalities and their causes to address deeper needs.

- **Embrace complexity** to remain patient and stay open to possibilities.

- **Seek liberatory collaboration** to reframe the user-designer relationship as one of partnership.

- **Build relational trust** to authentically collaborate and gain emotional trust.

- **Have bias toward experimentation** and action, and build to quickly think and learn.

- **Share your work humbly** without trying to convince users to provide feedback.

# Part Two

# The Design Thinking Process

*Chapter Three*

# The Five Phases of Design Thinking

Now that we have discussed the mindsets and values of DT culture, we will jump right into the inquiry-based process of DT. As stated earlier, the DT process applies transdisciplinary knowledge/skills with creative practices to collaboratively discover empathetic insights, generate and explore radical ideas, and create, test, and improve tangible outcomes. These outcomes could bring meaningful change to people's lives, improve real-world experiences, or solve complex problems.

The DT process provides students with a sense of comfort and hopeful confidence when faced with complex challenges. They understand that they might not have the knowledge and skills of an expert in a given topic, but as design thinkers, they have the tools to learn, be creative, and collaboratively produce innovative solutions to these challenges; they can be experts in the design process.

The process of DT includes five phases:

**1.** Empathize

**2.** Define

**3.** Ideate

**4.** Prototype

**5.** Test

In this section we go through the process in a linear fashion for clarity; however, there is no set progression in using these phases. Your students will jump from one phase to another in a nonlinear manner at any given time, based on need. For example, after testing a prototype and gaining feedback in the testing phase, a student might identify a new design insight and jump back to the define phase to revise her problem statement, then go back to the prototype stage to start building a solution based on the new problem statement. Many of your students will hit different phases multiple times during a project. In my elementary classes, I teach the process linearly so that they get a foundational understanding of each phase as well as the transitioning between them. Once they have a good understanding of each phase, students may jump between them. In middle and high school, it is important for students to personalize the DT process to fit their own design needs and preferences.

When I was first introduced to DT, I used the term "stage" rather than "phase" to describe the different parts of the process. I quickly found that my students started to misinterpret DT when I used the term "stage," which did not reflect the actual nonlinear and iterative aspects of the process. The term made the process seem like a step-by-step method, with each stage having well-defined barriers that prevented movement from one to another without the completion of the previous stage. For example, some students didn't understand that they could jump directly from the empathize to prototype phase if they wanted to communicate an idea visually through a tangible object. They thought DT required them to go through the define and ideate phases before creating any prototypes.

The term "phase" suggests a random, cycling quality to the movement between the different parts of the process. According to Tim Brown, phases are best thought of as a system of overlapping spaces rather than a sequence of orderly steps. He explains, "Projects may loop back through these spaces more than once as the team refines its ideas and explores new directions." These spaces give students the option to change their thinking and practices during any point of the DT process.

Additionally, the term "phase" alludes to what students will be doing in each of these spaces. Defined as "a short period of time during which a person behaves in a particular way," "phase" alludes to specific behaviors and practices that students will be applying in each of these spaces.

Each of the next five chapters will be dedicated to one of the five phases to provide a deeper understanding of each phase, with project examples that illustrate the behaviors and practices, as well as strategies and activities that will help your students be more successful. As a reminder, for students to use the DT process to its fullest potential, the learning environment must promote/develop a culture that is favorable to creativity and innovation as discussed in Chapter 2. Additionally, the learning environment must incorporate projects that simulate real-world scenarios or directly connect to the work that is being done by professionals outside of the classroom, which we will discuss in Chapter 4, under the Projects section.

*Chapter Four*

# Empathize Phase

*"We call this 'empathy,' and it is perhaps the most important distinction between academic thinking and design thinking. We are not trying to generate new knowledge, test a theory, or validate a scientific hypothesis—that's the work of our university colleagues and an indispensable part of our shared intellectual landscape."*

—Tim Brown, author of *Change by Design*

The empathize phase involves students focusing on and learning about the people they are designing for, as well as the context of the design challenge. It is what makes the DT process so human-centered. Students gain a deep understanding of the needs and wants of the end users, the people who will be using the solution designed to solve a problem or improve a real-world experience. In empathy work, students take specific actions to get to know, understand, synthesize, and share the feelings, values, and experience of the end user. Tim Brown describes empathy work as the "effort to see the world through the eyes of others, understand the world through their experiences, and feel the world through their emotions."

Students can gain empathy by engaging in interviews, observations, immersive experiences, and research. These types of empathy work can be daunting, especially for younger students, but with a lot of practice and the use of different strategies, students can unlock insights that they will find useful to their design. Insights are understandings that can help students see things in a new light, help challenge existing ideas, practices, or protocols, and explain why people behave in a certain way. These unanticipated findings can inspire designers to develop new ideas for innovative solutions.

# Self-Awareness and Partnerships

As stated in Chapter 2, Liberatory Design is an adaptation of the DT process that focuses on equity-centered design. Prior to empathy, students need to be aware of their own identity, biases, emotions, and assumptions to establish a partnership with the end user. In one particular first-grade project when students were asked to design a tool that would help a classmate improve the experience of a specific family activity (Family Activity Tool, page 76), some of the students had trouble removing, or even noticing, their own biases and preferences when designing for another person. They had to practice self-awareness to include the end user in their design.

According to Piaget's theory, children at the age of six start to be less egocentric and gain the ability to see from someone else's perspective. They are beginning to empathize with others and learning to be responsive to the views and needs of their peers. Since they are in the beginning stages of learning how to empathize, many students create what they would like instead of what is needed for their classmate. One student created a strikingly attractive boat, but it was obvious that it included aspects that were particular to him. This bias in design is not only seen in first grade but in all grades. People in general (even adults) have a tendency to want to create based on their own experiences and what they are fond of.

Due to this self-centered approach to design, I had to reiterate continually that their job as designers was to create something beneficial for their end user. They had to practice self-awareness and humility, turning their focus away from themselves to see that their end user was more important in context of the design challenge. I asked students struggling with egocentrism who their design was for and whether or not their end user liked the same things they did. Slowly they realized that they had their own preferences and biases that could hinder the process of creating the best tool for their classmate.

Since the end user was also designing a tool for their classmates, it was extremely convenient for them to test a tool, provide feedback and insights, and build upon ideas. David Clifford, Senior Learning Experience Designer at K12 Lab, explains that DT is all about partnership: "The more the designer/user become one and co-create, the more the design process becomes transformational, rather than transactional. And if it is indeed a partnership, then the learning and relationships never end. This is the beauty of equity-centered design thinking—it grows viral and inspires the humanity in everyone."

As an integral part of the design experience, end users were involved in every phase of the process. The partnership removed the idea of the lone genius designer solving the problems of the idea-less end user. One suggestion the d.school's K12 Lab gives to combat the unbalanced power dynamic of the designer and end user is to use the word "we" during conversations. For example, "How might *we* improve the tool so that it is easier to use?" The word "we" includes the end user in the DT process.

# Interviews

A group of second-grade students interview a real estate agent and the owner of a construction company located in the community to help them design a city plan.

Design thinkers gain a wealth of knowledge by interviewing the people they are designing for, as well as experts who are knowledgeable in the topic of the design challenge.

Interviewing end users gives students the opportunity to directly learn about what is essential to their user—their aspirations, motivations, and attitudes that could be powerful factors to the design of a solution. To do this well, an interviewer must listen without judgment or bias.

When interviewing experts, students quickly learn about a topic and gain valuable information regarding the design challenge. They can leverage a vast amount of experience and knowledge from someone who has already figured out what information is vital to the particular field of study, such as its history, current landscape, and context. It is the interviewer's job to seek insights that might be contained in the information through further questioning.

# Ask Broad Questions and "Why?"

In the City Plan project discussed on page 73, a second-grade team interviewed local community members to gain valuable insight toward designing an empathetic city plan. Ideally, generating the questions would be done by the students in their groups or as a whole class, but because of time constraints, the teachers prepared the questions for this particular project. It was also our responsibility to prepare our interviewees (local community members) as best we could for the interview. We made sure to provide them information about our project, their role in the DT process, the amount of time needed from them (10 to 15 minutes), and a preview of the interview questions that they would be asked.

## Interview Questions for Community Members

- What do you like best about your community?

- What is your daily schedule?

- Do you live/work in this community? How long have you lived/worked here? How do you get to work/home or out of this community?

- What has changed in this community since you first started working/living here?

- What do you like to do on your free time/breaks? What do you like to do in your spare time?

- What interests do you have?

- Why is this a good spot for your business? Is it or is it not?

- Can you describe a place that you love to visit?

- What do you like best about living/working near a school?

- What are your favorite foods? Where do you go for lunch?

The interview questions consisted of both specific and broad questions. For the specific questions, students asked "Why?" to find the causes of a community member's behavior or thinking. For example, when a student asked the real estate agent, "What do you like best about your community?" the agent explained that she enjoyed the location. The student then asked why the location of the community is favorable. He found out that she drove to other communities close by for the diverse selection of food and entertainment. This insight showed that community members were seeking out other areas for things they wanted in their daily lives.

Heidi Peterson leads a group of students to interview the owner of a coffee shop. Photo by Yoon Kim

The broader interview questions allowed students to gain information about the community members' lives, values, and habits. Students were able to find insightful patterns from the interview answers. By asking community members about their daily schedule, students learned that many of them worked for eight to nine hours a day. The students who lived in the area near school stated that their schedule consisted of studying in the morning, classes in the afternoon, and then more studying at home.

This information helped students realize that the community needed to provide its businesses and residents with spaces for relaxation and leisure activities.

Students learned that younger people enjoyed consuming media and hanging out with friends, while older people liked to spend their time doing some form of exercise, like golf or hiking. Even though these questions did not specifically relate to the community, the answers given provided powerful insights that could be used to design their city plans.

## Interviews through Stories and Conversations

One important objective in conducting an empathy interview is to encourage stories that show how the end users feel and think about the context of the challenge. Stories can unveil additional details that the prepared interview questions might not have. Since DT is human-centered, stories can also help students get to know their end users and place the storyteller not only at the center of the story, but also the design work.

First-grade student testing his Lego-grabber his classmate made for him.

First-grade students interviewing classmates to find valuable information that could help them in their design.

In the Family Activity Tool (page 76), students asked the following questions to elicit stories: "What's your favorite memory of your family activity? Can you describe it as a story?" Since our first graders were new to empathy interviews, we included these questions to explicitly require them to tell a story that they would enthusiastically enjoy sharing in great detail. As many of you know, young children are natural storytellers who are often willing to tell a story to anyone who will listen. For example, when asked to describe his family's fishing trip experience, one student said it was difficult for him to keep the slippery fish that he caught in his hands. From this valuable insight, the interviewee was led to design special gloves to help his classmate handle fish.

First-grade student testing his swimming footwear to see if it fits him.

Another objective of an empathy interview is to create a relaxed environment where interviewers can engage with end users through casual conversations. Empathy interviews can be overwhelming and daunting for both the interviewer and interviewee. When students feel that the process is too formal, they become more anxious and focus their concentration on asking their questions correctly instead of focusing on the answers to gain a deep understanding of the end user and his or her context. With the first graders in the Family Activity Tool, neither the interviewers nor the interviewees were being their natural selves.

Therefore, after asking their fixed questions, I asked the students to just *talk* to each other, to have a conversation to learn more about their classmate and their family activity. Students came up with findings and insights organically through casual conversations, which gave them the flexibility to ask additional questions about their classmates' thinking and feelings about their family activity. From this project, I've learned to avoid the term "interview" when teaching this type of empathy work. Instead, I tell students to "talk" to their end users, or have a "chat," "discussion," or "conversation."

By interviewing end users, the first-grade students were able to gain enough insight to design and build a tool for their classmate's family activity. We saw students creating swimming footwear that mimics a duck's webbed feet, a backpack for hobby supplies inspired by the pelican's large throat pouch, a Lego-grabber similar to a crab's claw to help clean Lego pieces, a fly-swatter for camping that looks like an elephant's tail, and a periscope to help a classmate see over tall objects.

## Listen and Don't Judge

Empathy interviews with end users were crucial to the students' ability to solve a school problem or improve a school experience. During Design Thinking Club, discussed on page 79, my students and I had a class discussion about the importance of listening without judgment, two principles of assuming a beginner's mindset.

At the start of the discussion, I introduced my students to an article called "Listening to People" that stated a person "remembers only about half of what he has heard—no matter how carefully he thought he was listening." We agreed as a class that effective listening would help them increase their knowledge and understanding of the end user and the context of the design challenge. However, if they only remembered 50 percent of what is said in the interview, then they needed to think of ways to become better listeners.

We discussed and listed the following strategies:

**1.** Be empathetic and truly care about what is being said.

**2.** Catch yourself not paying attention and direct your focus back to the interviewee.

**3.** Focus on the interviewee's answer without judgment, suppressing your inner critic. Many times, students inadvertently try to suggest specific answers that go with their own opinions, beliefs, or ideas. Instead, students should listen quietly to the answer, and only respond to clarify the answer.

All of these strategies required students to change their mindset before stepping into their empathy interview.

## Designing Questions

To prepare for an interview, have students brainstorm prospective questions to encourage answers significant to their project. For example, in the Festival Parade Floats project (page 85), students created questions designed to provide information that would effectively inform people about the festivals as well as ignite feelings associated with the festival.

When creating questions, it is vital to also think about sequencing, or placing questions into a specific order, as well as grouping them into general topics. This helps the interview feel more like an organic conversation. For example, in this project, students asked what the festival is about, why people celebrate the event or how it originated, and how people celebrate the festival. Finally, they asked questions that incited the expert to share opinions and stories from their own experiences.

Angie Bohcali shares her expertise with the fourth-grade students during an interview about a holiday festival.

Another key aspect of empathy interviews is note-taking, both through written words and with sketches. The information recorded during interviews will be analyzed and synthesized into insights that will help establish the problem statement specified in the define phase. Our students learned that note-taking requires them to write down any information that might be useful, and to write down exactly what is being said so that no insight is lost due to interpretation. Additionally, note-taking is a great way to help students stay focused during the interview process.

There will be times when you will need to remind your students to write down notes. I found that some students were forgetting to write down what was said because they were caught up in the interesting things the experts were explaining.

## Interview Rules

Here are some of the interview rules that one fourth-grade class came up with before their expert interviews.

**1.** Don't get distracted.

**2.** Be polite and respectful (listen).

**3.** Speak clearly.

**4.** Don't interrupt.

**5.** One person ask questions at a time.

**6.** Ask "Why?" politely.

**7.** Take notes and sketch information.

## Interview Principles

- Ask broad questions and "Why?"
- Incite stories.
- Have a conversation instead of an interview.
- Listen and don't judge.
- Take detailed notes.
- Deliberate in developing and sequencing questions.

# Creating Interview Opportunities

To create interview opportunities, students must first identify who the end user is in their design challenge. After identifying the end user, the teacher can contact them to see if interview sessions can be set up. Older students can find their own end users to interview, but they will need to be screened by the teacher for safety purposes.

These interview sessions can be done face-to-face or through online video chats with tools like Skype and Google Hangouts. Following the logistics of scheduling interview sessions, the teacher will facilitate generating open-ended questions that will provoke insightful storytelling, feelings, and emotions from the interviewees. These set questions will then be provided to the interviewees prior to the session.

For face-to-face interview sessions, it is important to keep the number of students interviewing one person to a minimum; assign a maximum of five students per interviewee. Too many interviewers can be overwhelming for the participant, and some students can get distracted, bored, or unmotivated because they don't feel like they are contributing or being part of the interview process. To combat the issue of participation (or lack thereof), every student in an interview group will have a role in note-taking and asking questions. It is crucial for all participants to feel comfortable and engage in relaxed, friendly attitudes. This will allow them to be more creative with follow-up questions, and the interviewee to be more open to share their opinions, feelings, and stories.

Via video chat, Christine Canales's fifth-grade class learns how Jack Andreasen and his team is designing a way to put carbon in the atmosphere back into the ground through carbon sequestration.

For expert interviews, students and teachers must identify the type of expert they would like to learn from. This will depend on the project. What subject areas does the project entail? What topics in each subject area are key to the completion of the project? After identifying the type of expert, the teacher (or the student, depending on the grade level and screening done by the teacher) will search for and contact an expert in the project topic. This can be done by researching online for possible experts from different parts of the world, or by looking for experts in their local community.

Experts around the world can be found in various online communities in different social media platforms. For example, you can find and contact experts through Google+ Communities, Facebook Groups, and Twitter hashtag feeds that pertain to the project's topic. You can send out a message to your online professional learning networks stating that you are in need of an expert who can answer your students' questions. For Twitter, check out the #dtk12chat feed to join a community of educators who use and teach design thinking in their schools. For more information about the community, visit www.dtk12chat.com.

When creating interview opportunities for the first time, I advise finding individuals in your school who would be considered experts by virtue of education, training, or experience. This would be a great first step in bringing in people from outside of the classroom who can contribute their knowledge and skills to your students. This will also help boost your confidence to approach experts from the community and other parts of the world to participate in the next project. If you are only able to connect with one expert, I recommend doing whole-class interviews where one expert answers the questions generated by the class.

# Observations

Observations are a key component to empathy work because they allow students to see their end user in the context of the design challenge. Students can see how their users interact with their environment, including what they do, how they carry out activities, why they do them in a specific manner, and what they are *not able to do*. The activities, behaviors, and feelings observed in this type of qualitative fieldwork can help students uncover insights. Therefore, it is crucial to have students visit and observe users in the actual environment where they will be using/experiencing the solution designed for them.

The empathetic outcomes of observations can be seen in the second-grade City Plan project (page 73), where students visited the community they were designing for. They walked through the community to observe the layout of residential/business areas, the people living and working in the community, the transportation and transport infrastructure, and the available land for new development. Students used their observational notes to see what needed to be improved in the community to increase efficiency, as well as what was missing that was essential to the happiness and well-being of the residents and business owners.

## Kids as Detectives: Observation Tools

As Tim Brown explains, "Good design thinkers observe. Great design thinkers observe the ordinary....Take a second look at some action or artifact that you would look at only once (or not at all) as if you were a police detective at a crime scene." Like detectives scanning a crime scene to find the motive of a crime and the criminal behind it, designers need to be meticulously observant. To help in this regard, they can take photos during a DT project. Photographs are great for documenting details that one might forget after an observation, capturing the ordinary that most might miss as well as providing a visual understanding of the context of the design challenge.

In the assembly portion of the Design Thinking Club School Solutions project (page 79), students went into their observations with a detective's mentality to find insights in the ordinary. During the project, they used their iPads to capture what they saw through photographs and videos. This provided them with an archive of observational findings that they used to uncover valuable insights back in class. Being able to use observational tools on the project allowed my students to identify and document the essential problem of the assembly experience: students getting to class later due to the traffic caused by only having one pathway for dismissal.

During the dismissal of the assembly, a third-grader and a fifth-grader observed that there was a huge traffic jam when leaving the Performing Arts Center (PAC) which resulted in a delay for students in getting to their classrooms.

Another observational tool is the d.school's What? How? Why? (WHW) tool. In the Toy Lab activity (page 87), second-grade students used this tool to help them design a toy for kindergarten students. The graphic organizer, divided into three sections, helped students progress their thinking to notice emotions and motives behind what they saw:

**1.** What? What are the kindergarten students doing?

**2.** How? How are they doing it?

**3.** Why? Why are they doing it this way?

Students answered these questions to find any insights, specifically related to what the kindergartners enjoyed doing and their preferences.

# Immersion

The third type of empathy work is immersion, the act of submerging one-self into a user's experiences. This requires students to do what the users do so that they gain a true understanding of the context of the design challenge. Immersion can come in the form of an analogous experience where certain aspects of the user's environment are simulated. For example, a designer could ride the back of a tandem bike to experience what it would be like to ride a self-driving car. Immersion can also be accomplished in the user's actual setting, physically experiencing the user's situation. For example, if a designer wants to improve the experience of waiting in line for an amusement park ride, he or she could simply go to an amusement park on a peak day and wait in a long line to empathize with a frustrated park-goer. The following projects illustrate how students gained empathy by physically experiencing the context of the user.

## Immersion Project Examples

As educators, we design learning experiences for our end users, the students. It is our job to design a learning environment and curriculum that meets their needs. Empathy can be a powerful tool to help us gain a deeper understanding of our students and be truly responsive to their needs. In Korea International School (KIS), a group of educators led by Brad Evans decided to gain empathy through student shadowing, an experience where teachers partner up with students, follow them throughout the school day, and experience everything through their perspective. The goal of the empathy work was to find insights that would help improve the student experience of the newly implemented Friday "skinny" day schedule.

In this high school, there are normally four 75-minute periods in a day, but the administrators decided to change the Friday's schedule to have eight periods, each period being 40 minutes long. The purpose of this Friday skinny day schedule was to provide teachers with an additional period where they could see all of their students. According to Aimmie Kellar, the high school associate principal, the teachers liked this idea because they would be able to see all their students right before the weekend. The new schedule would also bring equity for specific classes that had early dismissals due to sports activities and special events, and allowed flexibility for administrators to change scheduling for upcoming school-related events.

One high school teacher at KIS who participated in this immersive activity explained that experiencing the skinny day firsthand as a student was stressful because of the fast-paced nature of the day. All eight of the classes he attended started right away and didn't end until the bell rang. This was due to the fact that teachers were initially trying to cram their 75-minute lessons into 40 minutes. Combined with the short transition time, the varying distances between classes, and the inability to go to the bathroom, skinny day was an impediment to student learning. "I found myself literally running to East Asian Studies, and I was late for my own class [that I was teaching]," he wrote in his notes. "All I could think about was needing to go pee, and I didn't want to ask because I was already late. [As] the teacher, I had planned too much for a skinny day. When my class was over we had to really move to get from the sixth floor of the H Building to the sixth floor of the G Building for PE. At that point I just flat out told my PE teacher that I was going to be late. After changing and finally using the restroom, I noticed I wasn't the only late person."

Through immersion, teachers were able to learn about the needs of their students and make the appropriate changes to improve the skinny day experience. They realized their students were not benefiting from their brief, intensive lessons and needed to adapt them to be more appropriate for the skinny day periods. In this sense they realized that the schedule was not the only thing to blame for the hurried atmosphere, which was exacerbated by the structure of the lessons they were delivering. The administrators also added more time to the passing periods so that students would have more time to talk to teachers after class, go to the restroom, and make it to their classes.

Student shadowing also changed some of the opinions and perspectives of the teachers. Prior to the empathy work, many of the teachers assumed that tardiness was due to mismanagement of time, but they quickly learned that some of the late students were unable to make it on time due to other factors. They realized their previous assumption had also made it difficult for students to speak up and explain why they were late or needed to go to the bathroom; they feared that their teachers would not believe them or would hold them solely responsible. There was a sense that students were going through the day with the mindset of "This is just the way it is."

"In shadowing I noticed that oftentimes students didn't complain about things because they didn't even realize that it was abnormal," one teacher recounted. "When I saw really bad pedagogy—for example, the whole class being punished with more homework because too many students were late—I asked my shadow student what he thought about it; it hadn't even registered as a problem. Kids seem really good at adapting and normalizing things, so just asking him what should be improved in our school would never even get close to an issue like that." As designers ourselves, teachers need to make sure that students do not suffer from "badly designed" learning experiences that we have the ability to change. Without shadowing students, teachers would not have learned surprising insights and identified needs that required attention.

# Research

Research is a crucial type of empathy work that will most likely be involved in all of your DT projects. It is a great way for students to gain information about the design challenge as well as the users they are designing for. Provide students with learning resources, such as websites, nonfiction books, videos, and educational games that will help them acquire the knowledge and skills needed to solve the design challenge effectively. These learning resources should be readily available, not only in the empathize phase, but in other phases as well.

For example, in the testing phase, students might need do additional research on why their solution performed a certain way. In the ideate phase, research might bring more clarity before they actually build the prototype. It is important to provide a few prescribed resources that pertain to the topics in the design challenge because it can be a daunting task to find relevant, high-quality resources among the overwhelming expansion of information that is available online and in the library.

Ideally, projects should provide students the opportunity to interview, observe, or immerse with end users to gain true empathy. However, there will be times when this is not possible due to time, resources, or other factors. For those projects, research will be heavily relied upon in the empathize phase. Many of the projects that are showcased in this chapter started with research as the only empathy work done by the students. As we improved our projects over the years, we added more opportunities for interviews, observations, and immersion.

The Schoolhouse Design project, discussed on page 92, is an excellent example of a project that uses research as its main tool for empathy, but we hope to improve the empathize phase experience for this particular project by connecting our students with keypals from the region they are designing schoolhouses for. A keypal is a person who lives in another location, with whom students can share information or collaborate on projects. Our third-grade students would interview their keypals (end users) through emails, text messages, and/or video calls. Using the information they gain from their empathy work, students can design a schoolhouse based on the needs of their keypals that is suitable for the region's cultural practices, behaviors, and beliefs. Additionally, through this international connection, students can develop cultural competence by learning to successfully understand and communicate with people from other cultures, think and feel positively about the differences between cultures, and learn about the diverse perspectives of different parts of the world.

While research is a powerful and valuable tool for students to gain an understanding of the people they are designing for as well as the context of the design challenge, in human-centered design, it is more meaningful if students engage with real people to gain empathy, learn about their needs, and find out what is valuable to them.

# Empathy Map

The **Empathy Map** is a graphic organizer that visually displays and classifies the information captured during empathy work. During interviews, observations, and immersion, students record their findings in their map and classify them into seven empathic areas of focus, all in the perspective of the user. Created by Dave Gray, the founder of XPLANE, a consulting company, the Empathy Map was originally a business toolkit to help organizations gain a better understanding of their customers and their experiences. However, this tool is a great way for students to organize their findings, consider the motivations behind observed actions, and easily identify needs and insights.

**1.** WHO are we empathizing with? In this section, students identify the person or group of people they are designing for, the context of the design challenge, and the role of the user(s) in the context.

**2.** What do they NEED to do? Students list what their users need and want in regard to the design challenge. This includes tasks that their users want to accomplish and decisions they want to make. Additionally, students create criteria of what their users should be able to do to be successful in the design challenge. This section brings clarity and purpose on what they are trying do to help their user(s).

**3.** What do they SEE? These findings are based on what the user sees in the context of the design challenge, in their physical environment, as well as outside of these areas that might be influential to them.

**4.** What do they SAY? Students record what they hear their user say that might be influential to the design process, as well as what they imagine their user saying.

**5.** What do they DO? Students identify all the things that their user does in the context of the design challenge and in their daily life. They can also list some behaviors that they imagine their users to do.

**6.** What do they HEAR? These findings are based on what the user(s) hear from others, the people around them, or what they hear secondhand.

**7.** What do they THINK and FEEL? Students list what their user(s) fear, are frustrated with and anxious about, as well as what they need, want, and hope for.

According to Dave Gray, the first two questions identify the goal of the activity and clarify the context of the design challenge. The following four questions focus on the observable experiences of the user that allow students to walk "a mile in their shoes." The final question is considered one of the most important parts of the map because it requires students to imagine and find out what their user is thinking or feeling—the most significant action one can take to empathize with someone.

The version on page 71 is a combination of the K12 Lab (goo.gl/Cor8c4) and Gray's Empathy Maps (goo.gl/EKnM3U).

Name: _____ Date: _____

## EMPATHY MAP FOR STUDENTS

### 1. Who
Who are we empathizing with? What is the situation they are in?

### 2. Need to Do
What do they need to do? What do they need to do differently? What job(s) do they want or need to get done? What decision(s) do they need to make? How will we know they were successful?

### 3.See
What do they see? What do they see in their environment? What are they watching and reading?

### 4. Say
What do they say? What can we imagine them saying?

### 5. Do
What do they do? What actions and behaviors did you notice? What did they do today? What can you imagine them doing?

### 6. Hear
What do they hear? What do they hear others say? What did they hear secondhand?

### 7. Think and Feel
What are the thoughts and feelings that motivate their behavior?

What are their fears, frustrations, and anxieties?

What are their wants, needs, hopes, and dreams?

## Finally, find <u>Needs</u> and <u>Insights</u> of your user.

I cannot stress enough the importance of empathy in the DT process and how much it affects the quality of your students' work. I have seen first-hand how empathy work provided my students with insights that would never have been discovered without it. I've seen instances where my elementary school students produced higher quality products than secondary students who were given the same design challenges, simply because the empathy phase is the mainstay of DT work that allows students to value others' perspectives. Design thinkers understand that insights that might solve the problem can be spotted by someone who has the problem. Our students just have to discover how to empathize.

Once students finish their empathy work, they can proceed to identifying the needs and insights from the information they've collected. In doing so they can generate a problem statement that will guide their decision-making and actions, with the perspective of the user and their needs in mind.

# Projects

*"For the students who are the professionals of the future, developing the ability to investigate problems, make judgements on the basis of sound evidence, make decisions on a rational basis, and understand what they are doing and why is vital. Research and inquiry is not just for those who choose to pursue an academic career. It is central to professional life in the twenty-first century."*

— Angela Brew from *Transforming a University*

## City Plan

### Driving Question

How will you as urban planners design a city plan to improve the local community?

## Summary

Our second-grade students took on the role of urban planners, using DT to develop city plans that would improve their school's local community.

## Empathy Work

Students identified their end users to be the community members that live and/or work near their school. To connect the students with the community members, our team asked Yoon Kim, a parent of one of our second-grade students and the former Parent Teacher Organization (PTO) president, to contact and visit community members to see if they would be interested in participating in the project. She was able to enroll the help of the manager of the Mercedes Benz dealership, the owner of a coffee shop, a real estate agent, the owner of a construction company, and the high school students who live in the local boarding school. Our goal was to make the interview session as painless as possible for the community members. They were willing to take the time to participate during their work and study hours. It was our responsibility to prepare our students the best we could for the interview. We made sure to provide community members information about our project, their role in the DT process, the amount of time needed from them (10 to 15 minutes), and a preview of the interview questions they would be asked.

## Class Work

In social studies, students learned how communities meet the needs of their members, providing them with spaces to live, work, play, and solve problems. In science, they learned about the different landforms in the community and how they could affect the design of their city plans. Since the local community extends from the bottom of a hill to the top, they learned that the land slowly changes due to erosion caused by wind and water.

Using all of this information in design class, the students prototyped solutions that slowed or prevented erosion that might damage the local community's farming areas and buildings. They came up with solutions similar to retaining walls, erosion-control ditches, pier foundation systems that anchor structures to the hill, geotextiles, drainage systems, and windbreaks.

Second-grade students testing their erosion solutions during the testing phase.

Windbreak that blocks the wind from eroding the soil.

Drainage system that collects water and directs it to the bottom of the hill.

Retaining wall that prevents erosion caused by water by holding the soil in one place.

## Presentation

At the end of the unit, students presented their work at the City Planning Expo. They showcased their city plans, their brochures that explained how their plan would improve the community, and their engineered erosion solutions. They also presented the city plan promotional videos that they created in technology class to target visitors and bring more exposure and businesses/residents to the community. Parents, teachers, students, local urban planners, and community members were invited to the City Planning Expo, which provided students with an authentic audience.

# Family Activity Tool

## Driving Question

How will you design a tool that will help your classmate in their family activity?

## Summary

Our first-grade students partnered up and designed a tool for their classmate. The tool needed to help their classmate improve the experience of a specific family activity or solve a problem found in the family activity. At the end of the unit, students gave their tools to their classmates so that they could take it home and use it for their family activity.

## Class Work

In social studies, students learned about the similarities and differences of families and what makes each family special and unique. One difference they found was the unique activities each family chooses during their leisure time. In design, students interviewed their classmates about the family activities they like to participate in. They then used their newfound insights to ideate, design, build, and test their classmate's tool.

Students also used the concept of nature-inspired design (biomimicry) by incorporating what they learned about animal and plant composition that helps them survive, grow, and meet their needs. The first-grade students learned that nature has been evolving and adapting to life on earth for billions of years. Designers and engineers mimic many of the strategies and structures found in nature to solve real-world challenges. For instance, engineers in Japan mimicked the specialized beaks of kingfisher birds that dive into water with minimal splashing to decrease the large boom sound of their high-speed trains when entering tunnels. MIT scientists and engineers are looking to create a material that will help capture water in arid climates by mimicking the bumps on the Stenocara beetle's super-hydrophobic (highly effective water-repellent surface) back, which captures moisture in the air into droplets on its surface for the beetle to roll into its mouth.

In design, we challenged the students to use what they learned in science to incorporate an external part of an animal or plant into their tool design. Finally, students used their writing skills to create narratives that recounted the sequential events of their classmate's family activity and describe the tool that would help solve a problem or improve the experience.

First grader adds feathers to her handmade apron to add more insulation and an additional protective layer when painting. She also added a pocket that mimics the pouch of a kangaroo to place her art supplies.

## Empathy Work

In the empathize phase, students partnered up with a classmate, and they interviewed one another for two 55-minute class periods. Again, the teachers generated the interview questions because it was the students' first time carrying out an empathy interview. However, even at this age, it is best to have students generate interview questions once they have some experience with empathy work. For younger students it is most effective to have group discussions and generate questions as a class with the facilitation of the teacher. Here are the questions students asked each other to learn about their classmate's family activity.

**1.** Can you describe what you do in your family activity?

**2.** What do you like about the family activity? What makes it fun?

**3.** How do you feel when you do the family activity? What emotions do you feel? Why?

**4.** Can you show me how you do the activity? What movements do you do?

**5.** What's your favorite memory of your family activity? Can you describe it as a story?

**6.** What makes your activity not fun? What is hard about the activity?

These interviews provided enough insight for first graders to design and build a tool for their classmate's family activity. We saw students creating swimming footwear that mimics a duck's webbed feet, a backpack for hobby supplies inspired by the pelican's large throat pouch, a Lego-grabber similar to a crab's claw to help clean Lego pieces, a fly-swatter for camping that looks like an elephant's tail, and a periscope to help a classmate see over tall objects.

# Design Thinking Club School Solutions

### Driving Question

How can you create a solution to a problem at school?

### Summary

These pictures illustrate how interacting with the end user helped the fourth-grade students design a desk organizer that improved Ryan Persaud's workspace.

The Design Thinking Club is an after-school club I offer that provides students the opportunity to design solutions to problems they might find at school. These solutions can come in the form of an improvement to a specific school experience, such as the welcoming protocol of a new student or conflict resolution during recess. Solutions can also be tangible products that solve a problem a student or teacher might have. Before the start of the first club session, I sent out an online survey to teachers asking if there were any problems that they would like students to solve or any school experiences that they felt needed to be improved. Students were then placed into groups and allocated a specific problem.

## Empathy Work

Empathy interviews with end users were crucial to the success of each group's ability to solve a school problem or improve a school experience. Before the interviews, we had a class discussion about the importance of listening without judgment—two of the principles of assuming a beginner's mindset.

Two groups were notably effective in listening to their end user(s) and understanding their context.

One fourth-grade group visited and interviewed Ryan Persaud, the assistant curriculum coordinator, and learned that he needed a way to organize his desk that was full of paper, folders, and books. Through the interview, the students learned about his current organizational system, the limited amount of work space, his specific preferences, and most importantly, his dangerous allergy to peanuts. They used this information to design a clean, minimalist desk organizer that took up very little space, stored numerous documents, folders, and supplies, and included a large image that discouraged any peanuts in the area.

A group of fifth graders visited Stacy Trinh, a third-grade teacher who needed a footstool to help her add decorations and student work to the walls of her room. In her interview, students learned that the footstool needed to be safe and convenient to use, fit in between desks, and easy to maneuver. As a result, the fifth-grade students added wheels to the bottom of the footstool and a PVC pipe handle for easy transport throughout the classroom. They also placed a barrier around the step of the stool for safety purposes. Both the desk organizer and the footstool were well-received by the end users because they were designed strictly based on their needs and wants. During the interviews, students did not judge the answers given by the end users, but instead, humbly listened with a beginner's mindset and respected the interviewee's concerns.

The fifth-grade students present the footstool prototype for the third-grade teacher to test.

Two specific projects during the club benefited from observations. One project, similar to the footstool and the desk organizer examples, illustrates how tangible products can help solve a specific problem. Tara Verenna, the director of teaching and learning, asked our fourth-grade students to help improve the Center for Teaching and Learning (CTL) space, an area where teachers can come in for collaborative work and professional development sessions. She requested that the students help make the CTL a more comfortable place for teachers to learn. She also added, "We want to make sure that all supplies, materials, and learning resources are easy to access and organized."

Fourth-grade students interview Tara Verenna to find ways to improve the Center for Teaching and Learning.

The second project illustrates how designed solutions can help improve a real-world experience. Leann Norton, a second-grade teacher, asked our students to help improve seating and dismissal during assemblies. "At the moment, there are no assigned spots, and some grade levels are too big for certain areas," explained Norton. She continued, "How can we organize the PAC [Performing Arts Center] to be the most efficient use of space while keeping like grades together?" A third grader and a fifth grader partnered up to help Ms. Norton design a solution.

Leann Norton asked students if they could help the PAC become a more efficient space.

Before visiting the sites of the above design challenges, I introduced the students to the idea of design thinkers conducting themselves as detectives during observations. I began by showing them a portion of a TED Talk recommended by my co-teacher, Heidi Peterson, called *The First Secret to Great Design...Noticing*. In the presentation, engineer and inventor Tony Fadell explains how people get jaded by bad design. To illustrate this point, he told the story about stickers found on fruit that allow for faster checkout. However, these stickers' design flaw is that you can't just pick up the fruit and eat it; you have to look for the sticker and repeatedly dig at it until it comes off, sometimes damaging the fruit you are looking forward to eating. The first time people experience this, they probably feel frustrated, but as they come across this bad design more and more, they feel less frustrated, to the point where they don't have any feelings toward it at all. However, design thinkers are different. They see everyday things that the majority of people get used to, and try to improve upon them, or find a problem that needs to be solved.

When our first group of fourth-grade students visited the CTL, they observed that there was insufficient space between the tables, especially in the middle of the room. As kid detectives, they found it difficult to get through the chairs, particularly when people were sitting in them. Additionally, they saw that an office supply station took up a large amount of space against the wall. Using their devices, students took photos to reference during their work in class.

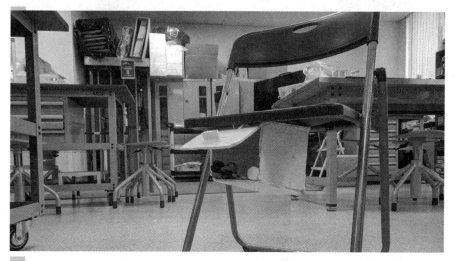

This prototype allows office supplies to be stored under all the chairs in the CTL.

Using what they discovered in their observation, the fourth graders decided to build a tool that would provide storage for school supplies that would eliminate the office supply unit against the wall without taking up additional space. They produced a storage container that holds office supplies and would be placed under each chair in the CTL. This allowed teachers to easily access office supplies whenever needed while freeing up space in the room. As a result, the tables could be placed farther apart, permitting teachers and students to easily maneuver through the aisles between the tables.

Danielle Rich, the elementary principal, provides our young design thinkers feedback for their assembly dismissal proposal.

The second group, whose challenge was to improve the assembly experience, took their iPads to an assembly to capture anything they noticed to be interesting. What they found was that there was no protocol for classes exiting the Performing Arts Center (PAC). Additionally, there was only one exit for 24 classes to take in the lobby to get to their classrooms. This created massive traffic in the lobby area with a few classes trickling through the one exit at a time. In our next club session, we visited the PAC to better observe the environment and found that there were doors in the front of the PAC that provided another route to the classrooms. Through their observations, the students devised a proposal plan that included new seating arrangements for each class, a protocol for students exiting the PAC, and the use of two additional exits that decreased the amount of traffic found in the lobby. The third- and fifth-grade students presented their proposal to their administrators, and their plan became part of the assembly protocol and implemented into the next assembly.

# Festival Parade Floats

### Driving Question

How will you as float designers build a model float that celebrates a February holiday?

### Summary

During the winter months, our fourth-grade students designed a mechanical model of a parade float for one of the following festivals based on the world language class they were in: Carnival in Spain, New Year's in China, and Mardi Gras in France. Students paired up to build and program their mechanical float models using a microcontroller called Hummingbird Duo and the Scratch programming language. Their goal was to help the school community gain an understanding and appreciation for each country's festival, as well as ignite wistful, evocative memories of past experiences for those who have actually celebrated the festival.

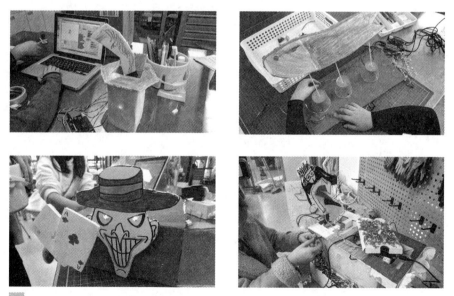

Here are some examples of mechanical floats that the fourth-grade students built and programmed for their festivals.

Students interviewed experts to learn about the festivals they were creating floats for. The elementary world language team, consisting of Chaoran Yao, Diana Caudill, and Karen Luu, arranged for themselves as well as the middle and high school world language teachers to visit the students for expert interviews. Through these expert interviews, students gained valuable information about their assigned festival.

Students learned about the history of the festival, how it started, and the story behind the celebration. The experts described the different traditions and activities, as well as their backstories. Students also learned about the various objects that represented the spirit of the festival: the festival's colors and the meaning behind them, the associated food and attire, and the folkloric figures associated with the festival. To elicit stories, experts were asked to describe their favorite experience and youngest memory of the festival.

# Toy Lab

## Driving Question

How will you as Toy Lab inventors design a nature-inspired toy for kindergarten students?

## Summary

Students created kindergarten toys that mimicked seed dispersal or plant pollination.

In the beginning of the year, our second-grade students took on the role of inventors for IDEO Toy Lab, a division of IDEO that designs toys and mobile apps inspired by kids' curiosity, imagination, and the desire to play and learn. Toy Lab has worked with the likes of Sesame Street, Fisher-Price, and LeapFrog. It has designed apps that range from teaching children dance choreography to helping relaunch the iconic stereoscopic toy, View-Master, to include a 360-degree virtual reality experience.

## Class Work

Students began the project in social studies, learning how community members have an important role in the community and the responsibility to make a positive impact.

The students studied famous inventors who made a huge contribution to society by addressing specific needs, learning about the characteristics and dispositions that help inventors make amazing creations. In science, students learned about the different ways seeds and pollen are transferred by plants and animals from one place to another for plant propagation. In design class, students used the insights found in empathy work to generate possible toy prototypes. They then built and tested their toy prototypes with the kindergarten students.

During the ideation phase, students incorporated their knowledge of seed dispersal and pollination into their toy solutions. For example, one student created a game where players throw metallic balls that stick onto a target using Velcro to earn points. The game mimicked the way bur, a part of the plant that contains seeds, sticks onto the fur of animals with its small hooks so that it can disperse seeds to another location. Another student created a toy that produced beautiful art with glitter. First, kindergartners glued parts of the paper that they wished to get glitter on. Next, they poured glitter into a paper cup that had small holes at the bottom. Then, they used the cup to sprinkle glitter on the paper for a colorful, reflective picture. This toy mimics wind pollination, where plants produce light, dry pollen that is carried away by wind to be captured by female structures on wind-pollinated plants. This toy actually demonstrates how most of the pollen goes unused by drawing attention to the misdirected glitter left in the plastic container.

Finally, the toy inventors used their informational and procedural writing skills to create a user manual, providing step-by-step, detailed instructions on how to play with the toy.

### Empathy Work

The kindergarten and second-grade teachers coordinated a class period where our toy inventors could make observations of their users. During the observation session, the second graders watched and listened to the kindergartners playing during a free-choice period, when the kindergartners chose between different stations with activities related to the content they were learning in class. Students observed how their kindergarten schoolmates completed tasks, physically played their games, expressed emotions, and interacted with their classroom environment.

# Breakout EDU Game Design

### Driving Question

How can you design a Breakout EDU game that your schoolmates can play during indoor recess?

### Summary

Fifth-grade students designed a Breakout EDU game. It is a game where the goal is to solve a series of challenges, riddles, and mysteries to "break out" of the classroom before time runs out. The game incorporates locks and boxes that contain clues, riddles, mysteries, or prizes. Students need to solve challenges to unlock the locks to retrieve valuable information or important artifacts. James Sanders, founder of Breakout EDU, created this learning platform based on his own experiences playing escape room games that similarly presented a secret plot, where players solve clues to get through multiple stages of objectives. He found that this type of game requires players to use what he calls the "4 Cs": critical thinking, collaboration, creativity, and communication.

### Class Work

Students began by building wooden locking boxes that would be used to hold clues and other artifacts for the game.

### Empathy Work

Students started the DT process by gaining empathy through immersion, playing a Breakout EDU game themselves to experience what their users would experience. Two games acquired from the Breakout EDU website were set up in the classroom for students to play: (1) the Minecraft-themed game Back to Reality and (2) the Star Wars-inspired game Attack of the Locks.

By playing the games, students were able to see how important it was for the clues to be intelligible and challenging, but at the same time enjoyable to solve. They realized that the game would not be appealing if the clues were too challenging or too easy. For one class, I mistakenly set up the clues and locks incorrectly. The students found themselves annoyed and exasperated, driving some to the limits of their patience and refusing to continue the game.

Students also learned that being provided a game theme, scenario, or storyline helped to get engrossed into the experience, motivating them to complete the narrative even with failed attempts to solve clues and open locks. By immersing themselves into the user experience, students gained a tremendous amount of information on how a user would think and feel when playing a Breakout EDU game, obtaining new perspective that influenced the work done in other DT phases. After capturing further insights during interviews with classmates and fourth graders, students designed their own Breakout EDU games and ultimately tested them out on classmates for feedback.

Fifth-grade students used wood-working tools and fasteners to build a wooden box for their Breakout EDU game. The box contained a lock hasp and a hinge to open and close its top.

Fifth-grade students creating their clues for their Breakout EDU game.

# Schoolhouse Design

### Driving Question

As engineers, how can you design a schoolhouse for children in a specific region?

### Class Work

In social studies, students learned about a specific region they wanted to design a schoolhouse for. They learned its physical and human characteristics, and its human/environmental interactions. They empathized with their end users, the school children in the region, by researching their distinct cultural practices, behaviors, and beliefs. In science students learned about the specific climate, weather conditions, and weather-related hazards in their region to inform the design of their schoolhouse.

Using what they learned in science and social studies, students designed and prototyped a model of their schoolhouse. They tested their schoolhouses in testing stations that simulated their region's weather-related hazard. For example, students who were designing a schoolhouse for a region in Bangladesh created solutions that would reduce the impact of heatwaves. They tested their prototypes using heat lamps. Students who focused on a region in Thailand tested their schoolhouse design in the "tsunami" testing station. Without researching these specific topics students would not have been able to gain the knowledge needed to answer the driving question.

*Chapter Five*

# Define Phase

The define phase involves students synthesizing the information they found in their empathy work to develop a problem statement. A problem statement defines what the meaningful challenge is all about and guides students through the DT process to a desirable solution. The statement identifies the user(s), their needs, and any insights that can provide design opportunities.

According to the K12 Lab, needs are the user's human emotional or physical necessities and desires that come in the form of verbs. Needs tell you what the solution will do for your users or what they will able to accomplish with the solution, not what the solution exactly is. Insights, on the other hand, are "remarkable realizations that you could leverage to better respond to a design challenge."

# Synthesis: Finding Needs and Insights

Now that your students have captured their learning in their WHW tool (page 64), it is time to synthesize the findings into needs and insights. According to the Interaction Design Foundation, synthesis in DT "involves creatively piecing the puzzle together to form whole ideas, organizing, interpreting, and making sense of the data we have gathered to create a problem statement." It is a way for students to share the stories and observations found in empathy work and develop a summary that puts everyone on the team on the same page regarding the goal of the design challenge. The following are two methods that students can use to synthesize their learning as a team.

## Story Share-and-Capture

The Story Share-and-Capture tool, also developed by the d.school, involves students unpacking their observations and describing the important things they saw and heard onto sticky notes; each sticky note contains a short title that describes the story of an observation. After everyone in the team has placed their sticky notes onto a large poster or whiteboard, the notes are organized into different groups based on a theme or pattern. Recurring, prominent ideas can prompt discussions and reveal valuable user needs and insights. This activity is a great way for students to compare their observational findings and drive the emergence of new insights.

The second-grade students used this method to identify key insights from their observational findings in the Toy Lab project, discussed on page 87. By grouping their findings, they were found that the kindergartners enjoyed playing with construction toys because they were able to use their imagination to create physical things. They also found that kindergartners enjoyed being part of a story through role playing games or pretend play. During the observations, some kindergartners took on the role of characters in a house or grocery store storyline. Additionally, students observed that the kindergartners liked to draw pictures, but used stencils to draw many of their shapes. They became aware that the kindergartners were still developing their fine motor skills. By grouping their sticky notes, students learned that they needed to consider the kindergartners' preferences as well as their developmental skills when designing a toy/game for their end user.

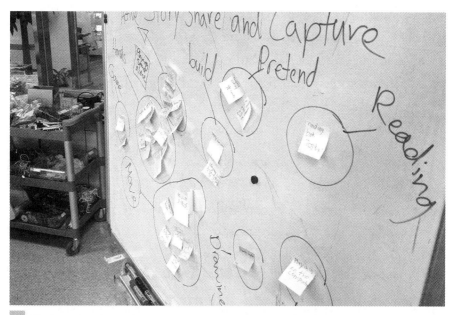

Each student in my second-grade class placed a sticky note that contained their finding onto my white board. I modeled the process of placing sticky notes into groups, and as a class, we identified any needs or insights gained from these groupings.

## Structuring Insights

As stated earlier, insights are realizations that you could leverage to better respond to a design challenge. An insight is composed of a finding, a detail learned during empathy work, which includes information on what causes the specific behavior. In his article "Synthesizing Insight," Matt Cooper-Wright, the Senior Design Lead at IDEO, makes the distinction between a finding and an insight by providing examples for a hospital scenario.

**Finding:** "Patients are often noncompliant. This makes their conditions worsen and [general practitioners] frustrated."

**Insight:** "Patients are so nervous during appointments that they don't listen to their doctors."

It is clear here that the insight sentence includes the finding as well as the cause of the behavior. The patients are not complying with the doctors (finding) because they are nervous during the appointments (cause of behavior). Students can structure their insights in the same way by identifying the causes of their findings. With younger students, it is best to model the process frequently, as well as find insights as a whole class. To better illustrate, here are some examples of findings from the City Plan project (page 73) that were transformed into insights.

| Finding | Insight |
| --- | --- |
| Community members drive to other nearby locations for food and entertainment. | Community members drive to other nearby locations (finding) because there are not a lot of options for food and entertainment in their area (cause of behavior). |
| Community members like to visit places of relaxation during weekends. | Community members like to visit places of relaxation (finding) because they are exhausted after working or studying for eight to nine hours per day (cause of behavior). |
| Older community members enjoy some form of exercise during their leisure time. | Older community members enjoy some form of exercise in their leisure time (finding) because they are more focused on their health than other people/groups (cause of behavior). |
| Businesses are doing well and remaining in the area for years with little turnover. | Businesses are remaining in the area for years and doing well (finding) because customers have easy access to the community due to the nearby highway (cause of behavior). |

By considering these insights, students gain design opportunities for innovative solutions to their city plans. These insights could lead students to design a city plan that provides a variety of food options as well as more places for entertainment. The city plan could also include sites for exercise (golf driving range, hiking trails, etc.), places for relaxation (spas, parks, gardens, etc.), and additional methods for customers to access the community more easily.

Cooper-Wright recommends asking a few questions to see if you have a quality insight. Does the insight inspire your students to start designing for the problem? Do you have a story that you can use to explain your insight? Is your insight interesting, surprising, or new? Does the insight have the potential to affect the design? And finally, is the insight relevant to the context of the design challenge? The process of synthesis and identifying insights can be difficult for students. Therefore, they will need the teacher to model the process and provide facilitation and feedback on multiple occasions.

# Problem Statement

After identifying the needs and insights of the user, it is time for students to develop an actionable problem statement that will drive inquiry and guide design work for the rest of the challenge. The problem statement states who the students are designing for, brings focus to the needs of the user, establishes a criteria for the success of the solution, and keeps every team member on the same page. It consists of three elements: the user, their needs, and user-based insights.

> "_____ (user) might need a way to _____ (user's need) that // because // but _____ (insights)."

In the first blank line, students would identify their user(s). This could include descriptive adjectives that specify exactly who they are designing for.

It is important to note that a problem statement is different from the driving questions we saw in the previous projects in Chapter 4. The driving question introduces the project that students will be working on.

It describes the purpose of the project and is phrased in an engaging, thought-provoking way to capture the interests of the students. The problem statement, on the other hand, is developed by the students after the driving question has been introduced, and after the students performed empathy work to gain an understanding of their end users. It is developed based on the parameters of the project and the needs and insights gained in the empathize phase.

Additionally, problem statements should not be too specific. Specific statements will lead to a few options for solutions, whereas open-ended questions will lead to more possible solutions.

Here are some possible problem statements from the projects discussed in Chapter 4, illustrating the user + need + insight structure.

## City Plan

- Residents (users) need a way to access a greater variety of restaurants and entertainment (need) that does not require them to drive to other locations (insight).

- Business people and students (users) need a way to rest and relax (need) because, surprisingly, they work or study for eight to nine hours each day (insight).

- Older community members (users) need a way to exercise (need) because they are conscious of their health (insight).

## Toy Lab

- Kindergartners (users) need a toy or a game (need) that incorporates activities that they enjoy playing (moving toys, pretend play, building things, etc.) and are appropriate for their level of fine motor skills (insight).

## Design Thinking Club

- Mrs. Trinh (user) needs a tool to put up displays onto her wall (need) because of her height, but she will need it to be safe and portable for small spaces (insights).

- Mr. Persaud (user) needs a way to organize his desk (need) because of his numerous documents and office supplies that cover his workspace, but surprisingly, it should deter people from bringing nuts in his office due to his allergic reaction (insights).

- Students and teachers (user) need a way to leave the Performance Art Center and get to their classes faster (need) because massive traffic forms in the lobby, surprisingly due to there being only one lobby exit for 24 classes to use (insights).

## Family Activity Tool

- Alex, who enjoys camping with his family (user), needs a way to repel flies (need) when he eats food, but to do it without killing them (insights).

## Festival Float

- People who've had exposure to the festival (user) need a way to experience a festival float (need) that will ignite wistful memories related to the festival from their past (insight).

# "How Might We" Question

Once students have developed their problem statement, they can transform it into a "how might we" (HMW) question. In doing so, students start altering their thinking from identifying the design problem to generating creative ideas to solve it. For example, here is one of the previous problem statements from the City Plan project: Residents (users) need a way to access a greater variety of restaurants and entertainment (need) that does not require them to drive to other locations (insight). The HMW question for this statement would be, "How might we develop a city plan that allows community members to stay in the area for a variety of food and entertainment options?" The "we" in the phrase can signify the team effort of the design work or can signify the partnership between the design thinker and the end user if it exists during the design process.

An HMW question helps students see that this is only the start of the creative process and ignites students to begin taking steps in using their imagination to develop creative solutions. In addition, the question suggests that the answer is unknown, requiring further design work, and the "we" in the question adds a collaborative aspect to the design work to come. This question provides students a transition into the ideate phase for brainstorming and generating possible solutions.

*Chapter Six*

# Ideate Phase

In the ideate phase, students use what they've learned from their empathy work to generate multiple solutions that have the potential to solve the problem statement, with their user(s) in mind. It's a transition from identifying and learning about problems to thinking creatively to generate solutions. The goal of this phase is for students to produce as many ideas as possible at the start, focusing on quantity, and then choosing the most intriguing and optimal ideas to move forward to the prototyping phase.

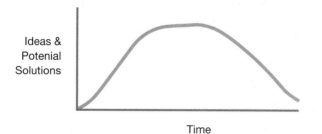

If we were to create a line graph that depicts the number of ideas being considered during the ideate phase, we would see something similar to a bell curve. The line would elevate as the team generates a large quantity of ideas, creating numerous potential solutions, and then gradually lower as the team evaluates their ideas, removing unwanted ones to end up with a few high-potential solutions.

# Demystifying Creativity, Innovation, and Originality

Ideation requires students to use their imagination and creativity. Creativity is the ability to go beyond existing ideas and create new ones. It is a frightening topic for many people, including students, because it is seen as an ability that only certain people are able to do naturally. However, this is a false notion in DT. David Kelley said that "creative confidence is like a muscle—it can be strengthened and nurtured through effort and experience." This quote suggests that everyone is creative and has the ability to be creative, but needs to work on it. In the documentary, *Design & Thinking*, Kelley states that "design is a sport where you have to actually participate." If design is a sport then a designer should train like an athlete. Athletes train their bodies to build strength and agility, practicing their sports skills through hours of repetition to compete with fierce opponents. In the same way, designers need to work out their creativity through training and practice. In the upcoming sections of this chapter, we will discuss different ways students can exercise their creativity and strengthen their creativity muscle.

Another reason people are intimidated by the topic of creativity is the myth of the lone genius innovator. The lone genius innovator is a person who is depicted as a creative type with the natural gift to produce innovations all by him or herself. However, this simple narrative contains two misconceptions. According to Eric D. Isaacs's article "Forget About the Mythical Lone Inventor in the Garage," the first misconception about these romantic myths is innovations don't involve a large number of people. Take for instance, Thomas Edison, the "lone genius" who invented the first electric light bulb. In his mythical story, Edison's stunning innovation was the result of more than 6,000 tests to find the correct filament material for the bulb.

However, this narrative often does not take into account that he was working with a team of 40 people in a large-scale research and development laboratory to find the correct filament for his bulb. He did not painstakingly perform 6,000 tests using different materials for 14 months on his own. With the success of the light bulb, he later built the Invention Factory to continue his invention work, which employed over 200 machinists, scientists, craftsmen, and laborers. This story shows how innovations do not always involve one person who acts alone; rather, the majority of innovations are the result of collaborative effort.

A big part of the ideate phase is the collaborative work that is done to generate to diverse, creative ideas. The majority of people do not see themselves as creative innovators because of these romantic myths. It is our job as educators to teach students that they are not learning to be the lone genius innovator but to develop into creative, collaborative problem-solvers.

The second misconception of the lone genius innovator is the notion that their creative ideas and innovations materialize from their own minds solely through their brilliance and creativity. However, this romantic depiction is not the whole truth. Yes, these innovators may be brilliant, but many times their innovations arise from the work and ideas of others who accompanied or preceded them.

In the *Smithsonian* article "Where Do New Ideas Come From?" Anthony Brandt and David Eagleman describe how most original ideas are derived from the work and ideas of others. One example they provide is Henry Ford's innovation of the assembly line for streamlining the process of building cars. Prior to his assembly line idea, "each vehicle was custom built, with different parts assembled in different places and then painstakingly brought together." Ford decided to instead build a factory that manufactured all the interchangeable parts and assembled the cars in one location, transforming the car industry forever.

However, Brandt and Eagleman pointed out that there was a long history behind Ford's assembly line idea. In the early nineteenth century, Eli Whitney designed weapons with interchangeable parts, allowing soldiers to repair broken rifles using the interchangeable parts of other weapons. Ford used this idea to manufacture interchangeable parts in large quantities that would be used in every car. Ford also looked to other industries for inspiration. He applied the continuous flow process of the cigarette factories to help rapidly produce products in one unceasing motion. Finally, Ford discovered the actual assembly line idea from the Chicago meatpacking industry, which used a conveyor to move carcasses through the meatpacking process.

This is not to say that individuals like Edison and Ford don't deserve their fame and recognition for their work in transforming the world. They absolutely do. However, it is important for our students to understand that these innovators collaborated with others and their innovative ideas stemmed from the ideas that were established before. Ford even admitted that his innovation was a culmination of the ideas and events that occurred prior. "I invented nothing new," he said. "I simply assembled into a car the discoveries of other men behind whom were centuries of work, and the discoveries of still other men who preceded them." Ideas are supposed to be taken, applied to other works, and improved upon for future innovations. Nikola Tesla, the inventor who designed the alternating-current (AC) electrical system, understood this very well. "The scientific man does not aim at an immediate result," he wrote in 1934. "He does not expect that his advanced ideas will be readily taken up. His work is like that of the planter—for the future. His duty is to lay the foundation for those who are to come, and point the way."

So how do we convince students with fixed mindsets that they are creative? How do we get those with little confidence in their ability to start being creative? The first step is to demystify the idea of originality because as Austin Kleon states in *Steal Like an Artist*, "Nothing is completely original." Kleon's truths about creativity as an artist can be applied to any field or aspect of life that involves creativity.

A person's creative work is constructed based on the work that came before it; it is a new mixture of different works or a new version of previous works. Kleon explains that once people realize this truth, they will give themselves permission to "steal like an artist" and utilize these "stolen" ideas to produce something new that is only part of a creative genealogy. "If we're free from the burden of trying to be completely original," Kleon explains, "we can stop trying to make something out of nothing, and we can embrace influence instead of running away from it." As an educator, help your students unchain their creativity by liberating them from the pressure and false notion of creating original ideas from nothing.

The second thing we can do to convince our students that they are creative is to actually have them produce creative work. They will see for themselves that they are capable of using their imagination and creativity to develop solutions to real-world problems. This confidence can be developed through the use of specific strategies and practices in the ideate phase. In this chapter, I will discuss methods to train your students' creativity and describe in detail the process in which students generate creative solutions. However, before this, we need to discuss the foundational principles of the ideate phase to help maximize your students' creative productivity.

# Ideate Principles

Establishing shared beliefs and guiding principles for creative work will foster a learning environment that is conducive to effective idea generation.

Part of the reason why I lacked success in my first attempts to incorporate DT into projects was not establishing these beliefs and principles for my students and the classroom. I learned that these beliefs and principles are essential for students to successfully apply DT practices and strategies in each phase. One resource that helped me greatly in developing an innovative culture was a video segment done by ABC *Nightline* look into how designers create better products for end users.

*Nightline* challenged IDEO with the most difficult challenge they could think of: redesigning the standard shopping cart in only five days. The video segment showed David Kelley and his team of designers visiting shopping centers, and interviewing customers and employees to empathize with the end users. They used what they learned to produce a shopping cart that was way ahead of its time.

The futuristic shopping cart was not a large basket on wheels, but instead contained removable hand baskets that allowed shoppers to leave their cart anywhere to go find different items. This would minimize the traffic created by shoppers going through the store with their large carts. Other features of the cart was the child two-seater with an adjustable tray that functioned as a play surface, wheels that turned 90 degrees to help shoppers maneuver in difficult situations, and most inventive, the high-tech scanner that allowed customers to check out without waiting in long lines. With all these innovations, the shopping cart still cost the same as the standard carts at the time. Most surprising is the fact that this shopping cart challenge was done in 1999. So how did IDEO produce such a cutting-edge product in just five days?

On day two of their design challenge, the IDEO team undertook a brainstorming session in a room that had different mantras posted on its walls. These innovation mantras or principles were the driving force of the brainstorming session, guiding the conversations, behaviors, attitudes, and decision-making throughout. During what IDEO describes as the "deep dive," where designers totally immersed themselves into the design challenge, they generated creative solutions within the framework of the following principles:

**1.** One conversation at a time

**2.** Stay focused

**3.** Encourage wild ideas

**4.** Defer judgment

**5.** Build on the ideas of others

In my experience, it is grueling for students (as well as teachers) to collaborate and brainstorm ideas without each person following or believing in the innovation principles above. Skeptical groups are unable to produce a large quantity of ideas and have trouble progressing in productive ideation work. These principles provide students a framework where they can collaborate and ideate effectively to advance closer to an innovative solution. In the next section, we will take a deep dive into the process of ideation, and also focus on specific projects that best illustrate each of these valuable principles.

# Pre-Brainstorming: Mindset, Warm-Ups, and Practice

Before students engage in ideation, transition their mindset toward practical optimism. A positive-thinking mindset is especially important in the ideate phase. According to Donna Wilson and Marcus Conyers's book, *Teaching Students to Drive Their Brains*, it can improve motivation and productivity, but most importantly, enhance creativity and problem-solving.

**Practical optimism** is a combination of positive thinking and practical beneficial action intended to bring positive results. In the ideate phase, practical beneficial action generates creative ideas that have the potential to solve the problem statement. This realistic, hopeful confidence about the future of their work allows students to believe that obstacles and failures are only temporary and can be altered to positive events by their own behaviors and actions. In contrast, a pessimist would see these obstacles and failures as permanent and pervasive. Practical optimism does not ignore the negative obstacles and barriers, but understands that these negative events bring new insights, learnings, and improvements. It also involves belief in one's own abilities and courage to develop a workable solution. Remind students, or have a class discussion, about how optimism could affect their ability to be creative.

Once students are in the right mindset, it is vital to have them warm up their brains before they brainstorm ideas with their team members. As mentioned before, the design process is like a sport. This is especially true for the ideate phase; an athlete wouldn't go straight into a game without stretching and warming up, so why have students ideate without preparing their brains for strenuous brainstorming? During my first experience with DT at the Beyond Laptops conference session, our presenters asked us to start brainstorming ideas that would help solve the problem statement that we created. I remember looking at my partner and thinking "where do we start?" Absolutely no ideas came to my head. I looked at my blank paper and then looked around at the other attendees. I saw that some of my peers had the same problem as I did; they looked lost and unsure how to begin.

I was also taken aback by my presenters' request to think up a large quantity of ideas. I was more comfortable in a faculty meeting setting where I would suggest a few ideas related to an agenda topic—having to be creative and think up bold, even unusual ideas, was a daunting task for me. I discovered that many of my students were also unable to ideate when I told them to "start being creative." I would announce to the class, "Okay everyone, go ahead and think up a lot of ideas!" Ideation is not an activity that people naturally excel in; it requires practice. Through my own experience and from watching my students struggle with the ideate phase, I learned that it is essential to give students the opportunity to practice their brainstorming skills and warm up their brains before they ideate. The following activities can provide students with these opportunities, as well as a chance to further practice the innovation principles.

## Getting Stuck with 30 Circle Exercise

In his webinar, *Design Thinking: Training Yourself to Be More Creative*, Stanford professor Bill Burnett explains that creativity is a "high-energy brain behavior that is not normal for most brains." However, Burnett believes that creativity can be learned, and since it is a high-energy brain behavior, training is required for people to perceive the world as creatives do. One of the reasons why people fear activities that require creativity is because of their disdain toward the feeling of being stuck. This feeling of being stuck happens when people don't know what to do next, don't know what decisions to make, fail to meet a goal, or in the case of the ideate phase, can't think up creative ideas. Burnett suggests people should train themselves to get *stuck* so that their fear will decrease as they get more exposed to this type of situation.

One activity Burnett recommends is the 30 Circle exercise, where a group or individual participants are given a sheet of paper with 30 blank circles. Their task is to take each blank circle and create something new. For example, I could take the first blank circle and draw lines inside it to make it look like a basketball. The objective of the activity is to try to create something new with as many circles as possible in two minutes, encouraging wild ideas throughout the time period. Obviously, no one in my classes has actually been able complete all 30 circles in the two minutes I have given them, but most importantly, they are all forced to experience getting stuck.

Before administering this activity with my third-grade students, I explain that my favorite part of being a teacher is witnessing their **aha moments**. These moments occur when students get stuck, when they are struggling with understanding a concept or the ability to do a skill in an activity. But in an instant, something clicks and they discover an idea or do something that they thought was impossible before. I tell students about my love for these moments to illustrate that their struggles will likely be met with a moment of clarity and satisfaction.

According to Burnett, it is important to teach students that "being stuck is a gift because right around that *stuck* is that *aha moment*." He states that these moments trigger high levels of activity in the brain, releasing endorphins and dopamine that make the experience pleasurable. Help students realize that as designers, we tackle problems that we initially don't know how to solve. Because of this, we will experience many moments of being stuck, but an aha moment could be just around the corner.

Name: _____ Class: _____

**30 Circle Exercise**

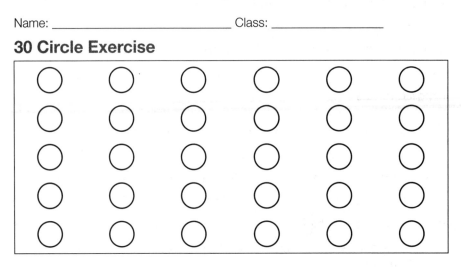

# Improvisation with Word-Ball and Party Planner

Burnett also encourages students to practice improvisation to improve their brainstorming skills. Improvisation is the act of making things up on the spur of the moment without any prior preparation. For example, in improvisational theatre, the actors of the live show spontaneously create the story, scenes, characters, and dialogue on the spot. These theatre elements are created based on what the previous actor developed, or even what the audience suggested. Another actor takes what he or she sees and hears and continues with the idea to further develop the story. Improvisation is a great way to simulate how your team of students should brainstorm and collaborate to work toward one common goal. It allows them to practice building upon the ideas of others, and actively engage in listening, thinking, and creating alongside their teammates.

One improv activity I use in my classroom is **Word-Ball**. I found this activity in the book *The Achievement Habit*, authored by Bernard Roth, one of the founders of the d.school. Roth explains that the purpose of the activity is to have the ball continuously move from one student to the next. In addition, the student who throws the ball needs to introduce a new word to the group. The student who catches the ball needs to repeat what was said and then instantly introduce another word to the group that immediately pops up in his or her head.

There are a few differences in the way we conduct Word-Ball in my class. First, the person throwing the ball makes an effort to relate their word to what was said by the previous person to practice the skill of building upon the ideas of others. Second, we see how long it takes for every person in the class to engage in throwing, catching, and introducing a new word. This requires the person who threw the ball to sit down immediately so that we know who already participated, and involves everyone in the class taking part in the activity. Additionally, we use an imaginary ball instead of a real one for our younger students so that their gross motor skills (or lack thereof) don't affect the fluency of the game.

Another improv activity I have used with my students is the **Party Planner**. It was introduced to me by Ellen Deutscher, an educator for over 20 years and a leading advocate for design thinking in education. In this activity, the group takes on the role of a party planner. One planner starts with a party idea, such as a party with a dinosaur/prehistoric theme. In the first round, the remaining party planners respond to the idea with a "Yes, but" response. This response includes the reason why the idea that they heard would not work or is not a good idea. So, for our example, a student might say, "Yes, but some of the children might be scared of these creatures because of their lizard-like features." At the end of this round, our party planners most likely have envisioned a lifeless party people would not get excited about or enjoy themselves in. Students realize that frequently using the "Yes, but" response stops the development of a great idea and halts the creative momentum that the group may have created. As educators, we experience this all the time in our faculty meetings where some of the teachers habitually respond with "Yes, but" responses, resulting in an hour of discussion with teachers leaving the meeting wondering if anything was accomplished.

The second round consists of students using the "Yes, and" response. Here students take the idea of the previous planner and build upon it, making the overall party idea even better. Let's say the first party planner suggests the following idea: "How about we have a party that includes showing a popular movie projected in the backyard?" The next party planner could add, "Yes, and maybe we could provide attendees a movie premier experience with a red-carpet arrival and 'paparazzi' taking their photos." As this idea continues to be built upon by each party planner, students start to see a drastic difference between the party idea they shared in the first round and the idea they shared in the second round.

Both the Word-Ball and Party Planner activities help students to practice their improv skills, which in the end will benefit their ability to effectively collaborate and brainstorm ideas with their teammates. According to Patricia Ryan Madson, a Stanford professor in the Department of Drama, a good improviser is a person who is "awake, not entirely self-focused, and moved by a desire to do something useful and give something back, and who acts upon this impulse." These activities require students to stay focused in what everyone is sharing, really listening to what everyone has to say. Their thinking and energy is focused on making their teammates' ideas better without making judgments on their quality. Most importantly, these activities provide practice and growth in their ability to spontaneously produce creative ideas.

Word-Ball takes elements of improv and gives students the opportunity to practice some of the ideate principles essential for collaborative and creative brainstorming.

## Teaching Ideate Principles through Disruptus

Heidi Peterson, my co-teacher in design, suggested playing **Disruptus** with the students after she'd played it over the school break. At the vacation lodging, she played the brainstorming game in teams with her friends, who were mostly educators. Heidi observed that some teams were able to be creative and come up with cool ideas as a team, while others had difficulty generating ideas collaboratively. It was clear that the team that conceived novel ideas was using some of the ideate principles.

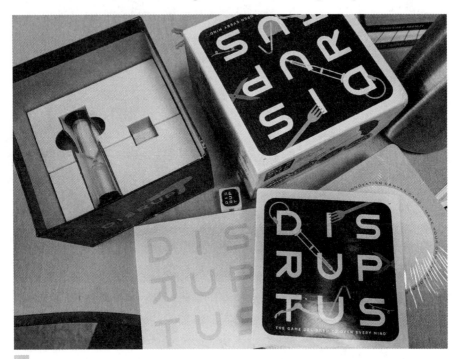

Disruptus is a game that allows students to develop their ability to use the ideate principles to generate creative ideas as a collaborative team.

The purpose of Disruptus is to have students brainstorm innovative ideas by looking at objects from different perspectives and thinking beyond the obvious. The game is based on the concept of **disruptive thinking**. According to the game manual, disruptive thinking is "looking at an object or idea and coming up with an entirely different way to achieve the same end." In his book *Disrupt: Think the Unthinkable to Spark Transformation in Your Business*, Luke Williams describes how businesses famously use this type of thinking to find the one thing they do that no one else does. Through disruptive thinking, a business "surprises the market again and again with exciting, unexpected solutions, produces an unconventional strategy that leaves competitors scrambling to catch up, turns consumer expectations upside down, and takes an industry into its next generation." Disruptive thinking is important in DT because it allows students to challenge their ideas, understanding, and expectations about the problem they are designing for.

In the game, students roll a die that features four different approaches to innovation: Create, Improve, Transform, and Disrupt. If students roll Create, they get to turn over two cards, each card containing an image of an object. Next, students get to use the different parts of the two objects to create something new. Let's say a student turned over a card with sunglasses and a card with a cup and a straw. The student could sketch a picture that attaches the straw to the sunglasses' frame to create a snorkeling device. If students roll Improve, they need to enhance the object on their card to make it even better. For example, if a student flips over a card that contains a hair dryer, he or she could sketch a muffler at the end of the hairdryer to weaken the sound of the device.

When rolling Transform, students get to think of another way to use an object on the card for another purpose. For instance, a plastic bottle could be used to create a sprinkler by poking small holes in it and attaching it to a water hose. Finally, for Disrupt, students will examine the function of an object and see if they could find a new way to achieve the same function. Turning over a card depicting an umbrella, a student would need to find a new portable way to prevent people from getting wet. He or she could sketch a hat and jacket that is made up of repellent material that bounces water off its surfaces.

After students play the game for the first time, provide them with some time to reflect on their experience, and discuss as a class what behaviors and thinking allowed or prevented their team from generating large quantities of creative ideas. During their first time playing the game, you will observe some teams encouraging wild ideas and building on the ideas of others, but also teams that are not focused on the topic at hand and have trouble generating ideas because of the judgment from their teammates. The ideate principles should emerge in the discussion through these examples, which will provide a great opportunity to transition into teaching students what these principles entail. Then, the next time the game is played, students will realize for themselves that applying the principles is advantageous to their team's success in the game. Enhance the learning during the game by modeling the behaviors of each principle and stopping the class when you see a great example of one of the principles being executed skillfully.

One third-grade student transformed this name tag label into a tool to help English language learners learn the names of different objects around the classroom.

Another important aspect of the game is the judge, who determines which idea is the best in each round. This aspect of the game allows students to practice their empathy skills. The criteria for the best idea is highly subjective. Students need to tap into the judge's personal opinions, perspective, values, and preferences to develop ideas that have a chance to win. However, students also learn that there is a balance in incorporating their judge's personal preferences with how useful the idea is to the judge. For example, students in Sarah Donaldson's third-grade class knew that their teacher loved to eat sushi. Some teams incorporated this preference into almost all of their ideas; however, none of their ideas were chosen because they were not practical to her. On the other hand, teams who were able to develop ideas that harmoniously combined her love for social justice with the object that was on the card were able to grab her attention.

# Divergent Thinking: Apple Devices for English Language Learners

Once students are in the right mindset, they will embark in the first stage of the ideate phase that involves creative brainstorming to generate ideas that will help solve their problem statement. This stage embraces divergent thinking where students are brainstorming as many ideas as they can, not judging the quality of their ideas, but thinking broadly and creatively to aim for a large quantity of ideas. This period of creative brainstorming involves the encouragement of wild ideas, the act of building upon the ideas of others, and the process of getting unstuck. We will discuss this part of the ideate phase through a project I did with my fourth-grade students.

Apple is famous for attracting millions of customers with their elegant products that combine simplistic design with great performance. Witnessing the excitement my fourth-grade students show for the company and its products, I decided to use their unit on energy to create a project based on the creation of Apple devices. I asked two friends who are Apple Distinguished Educators, Steve Katz and Tim Bray, to video chat with my classes and introduce the following driving question: How will you as Apple engineers design, test, and refine a voice recording device for English language learners?

Through the DT process, students had to empathize with English language learners and realized how voice recordings can help them improve their reading fluency, developing their reading rate, phrasing, pausing, and stress. In science, students learned how energy can be transferred from one place to another by sound, light, heat, and electric currents, and how it can be converted from one form to another. In design, students learned how Apple devices draw in millions of customers by incorporating simplistic, accessible, and sleek designs. Using the knowledge of multiple subject areas, students used the engineering process to design, build, test, and refine an "Apple" voice recording device.

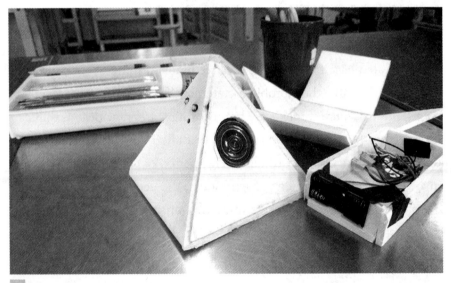

Students had to assemble electrical components to create a working voice recording device. They also designed the casing for their device using foam board and a precision knife.

## Quantity Over Quality

At the start of the ideate phase, students brainstormed ideas that would help make their device aesthetically pleasing and provide a great user experience for their end users. Before their brainstorming session, I reminded students that they were going for quantity and not quality, and encouraged them to think broadly in terms of their ideas. "For any ideas that come up in your brain," I told them, "sketch it out on your paper immediately. I want to see your whole paper filled with ideas. It does not matter if you think it is a bad idea. Just sketch it out!" I instructed them to sketch even bad ideas because this sustains a momentum of creativity that develops their natural flow, rhythm, and fluency in ideation. Interrupting the flow and momentum of creative thinking due to their fear of "bad" ideas is not productive to the brainstorming process.

We all have a tendency to critique our ideas and work harshly. The judgment of our own ideas stops us from gaining any creative momentum to produce a large number of possibilities. Students new to my class or with very little experience with the DT process were only able to sketch out one or two ideas for their Apple device compared to some of the "veterans" who had every space on the front and back of their paper filled with ideas.

The biggest difference between these students is their thinking. The newer students were afraid to put any of their ideas on paper because of their fear of being judged or seen as uncreative. Some of the newer students had a tendency to create detailed masterpieces that they spent their whole brainstorming session creating. You could even see the numerous erase marks that these students made when trying to perfect their drawing. As nice as these drawings were, they were still only one idea. Sketches are supposed to quickly and clearly communicate an idea, drawn rapidly and roughly so that students can move onto the next idea. To do this, students need to suppress their perfectionist propensity. It is better to end a 15-minute brainstorming session with 20 quick sketches than one masterpiece.

So why quantity over quality? I help students answer this question by drawing an example on the whiteboard of two students, one generating just a few ideas and the other generating a large quantity of ideas. Let's say the first student sketched three detailed ideas for their Apple device in 15 minutes while the second student sketched 14 ideas during the same amount of time. Based on this drawing, I asked my students to vote for the person they thought would produce more great ideas to take into the prototype phase. The majority chose the second student because they believed that the more ideas a person has, the higher the probability of producing high-quality, creative ideas. Yes, the second student might have more bad ideas, but he or she also has more radical, innovative ones. Going for quantity will already include quality ideas, but also have ideas that go beyond the obvious. Additionally, the second student has an opportunity to take the best parts of each idea and combine them to create one awesome solution, whereas the first student is limited in his design options.

This drawing demonstrates how generating a large quantity of ideas can lead to a higher number of good ideas and provide more creative opportunities and options. The stars and their size represent the idea and the quality of the idea. As you can see the first student has two great ideas, but the second student has five.

## Encouraging Wild Ideas

Going for quantity required the fourth-grade students to think beyond the obvious solutions or ideas for their Apple device. Students may have sketched out the obvious ideas initially, but as they continued, they started to generate bold, imaginative, and even wild ideas. Giving students the freedom and encouragement to come up with wild ideas can spark some surprising possibilities and inspire innovative solutions.

To illustrate how Apple implemented their wild ideas to create a smartphone that would revolutionize the smartphone industry, I showed the fourth graders an image of the iPhone 3G that was released in 2008. Students initially reacted to the "ancient" phone with bewilderment and disgust. They couldn't believe how different the phone was from the iPhones their parents owned. However, they were even more shocked by the image I showed them of an old Blackberry phone. I explained to them that the Blackberry phone model was the leader of the smartphone industry for almost a decade before the first release of the iPhone. In 2007, Blackberry was valued at $40 billion with more than one third of the smartphone market share in the US.

Apple changed all this with their new stylish iPhone that incorporated a simple, easy-to-use touchscreen user interface, an amazing Internet browser experience, and an innovative design that got rid of the physical keyboard and unneeded buttons. Apple was able to take their wild ideas—ideas that seemed impossible to execute, even for the people who built the phone—and bring them to fruition. In *The One Device: The Secret History of the iPhone*, Brian Merchant features some of the conversations he had with top Apple designers and managers who described the unsettling challenge of making the impossible possible. "I thought, *Yeah*, it seems kind of impossible, but it would be fun to just try it," said Bas Ording, the iPhone user interface designer. Andy Grignon, the iPhone senior manager, reflected on the enormity of project. "It was really intense, probably professionally one of the worst times of my life. Because you created a pressure cooker of a bunch of really smart people with an impossible deadline, an impossible mission, and then you hear that the future of the entire company is resting on it. So, it was just like this soup of misery."

Encouraging students to think up wild ideas increases the probability of coming up with a creative solution to their design problem. Yes, when introduced to DT for the first time, students will frequently come up with wild ideas that are not focused or relevant, but with practice, their ideas will become more innovative and applicable. It is a way of thinking that allows students to focus on being creative instead of the constraints that might be present. You never know, a wild idea could be exactly what is needed to solve a complex problem statement. It worked for Apple!

# Building Upon Ideas of Others through Plussing

When students build upon the ideas of their teammates, it adds to the creative momentum of the brainstorming session, creating an energetic environment for collective ideation. It is a strategy students collaboratively use to turn a good idea into a great one. In our design class, we use the **plussing** strategy to help students build upon the ideas of their peers. Popularized by Pixar Animation Studios, plussing is a strategy that is derived from three improv principles: (1) accept every offer, (2) use "yes, and" instead of "yes, but," and (3) make your partner look good.

According to Randy Nelson, the former dean of Pixar University, a professional development program at the animation studio, plussing is when a team member takes the work or an idea of another person and thinks, "Here's where I'm starting. What can I do with this? How do I plus this? How do I accept the offer and make my partner look good?" It is the open-minded act of taking an idea and making it better, continuing the creative conversation and momentum, and not shutting down ideas completely.

To demonstrate the plussing technique to my students, I draw a scenario on the whiteboard of two students in a brainstorming session. The first student shares an idea that she has, saying, "What if we did this?" "That's great! We could also add this to it," replies the second student. "Amazing! Yes, and how about we make it do this?" responds the first student. The idea that each person shares or adds on is represented with a star in a speech bubble. As the conversation continues, the stars (ideas) get larger, representing the growth and continuous improvement in quality and innovativeness of the initial idea. At the end of the drawing demonstration, the two students end up with a huge star, an idea that makes the first student look good.

In this illustration, each student builds upon the idea of the other person. They do this by accepting the idea, saying "yes and…" and trying to make their partner look good. The increase in size of the stars represents how the idea continues to improve as the students "plus" the idea multiple times.

During the brainstorming session in the fourth-grade Apple project, I provided students with plussing sessions. Students would share their ideas and have their partners plus them. As they plussed each other's ideas, I walked around the room to listen to their conversations and find a great example to share with the class. Once I found a great example, I stopped the whole class, described what I saw and heard, and focused the attention onto what made the group's plussing so effective. I pointed out how the students were deferring judgment of the ideas that were shared with them, not deciding whether or not the idea was good, but simply taking the idea and making it better. I also pointed out how students were finding the positives of an idea and then adding onto it through the use of positive language like "yes, and."

Since plussing involves the deferring of judgment and using positive language, it is also a great way for students to provide feedback to one another, not only in the ideate phase, but in the other phases as well. Ordinarily, feedback identifies weakness in an idea or piece of work; however, in plussing, students instead go straight to a suggestion that provides an alternative solution or improves the idea to turn its weaknesses into strengths. Like I mentioned before, many of us have been in meetings where teachers shoot down every idea by explaining why each one would not work, without providing any alternatives. We end up having discussions that go nowhere and don't result in any solutions, totally wasting valuable time that could have been spent on class prep. If you want to change draining, judgmental meetings into productive, positive ones, try incorporating the plussing strategy into them.

# Sharing and Capturing Ideas

There are different options for students to document and share ideas during the ideate phase. In the Apple device project, students brainstormed and sketched ideas individually onto their own sheet of paper. These sketches did not have to be sensational artwork, but needed to communicate the students' ideas. Once they were finished, they had the option to share their ideas with their classmates via a collaborative plussing session, improving their classmate's ideas and making them look good.

For group work, students visually display their ideas on one large sheet of paper. They use the ideate principle of "One conversation at a time" to share ideas with one another. Once a student has sketched out an idea, they can turn to their group, show them his or her sketch, and then explain how the idea works; no one may interrupt the conversation until the person has finished. This process of capturing and sharing ideas helps everyone know what ideas have been communicated, provides opportunities for the ideas to be plussed, and helps everyone in the group stay focused on the same page. Using one poster paper for a group to sketch and share ideas gives every student the opportunity to contribute in a safe, creative environment where everyone's ideas are seen, valued, and listened to.

You can also use sticky notes to capture and display ideas during the brainstorming sessions. Sticky notes allow students to focus less on how well they sketch their ideas, and more on their substance and how to communicate their ideas well. Perfectionists unable to draw their time-consuming artwork onto the smaller-sized sticky notes are forced to move onto their next idea. This tool also encourages students who feel unconfident in their sketching abilities to share their ideas since they can rely more on their writing or verbal skills. Additionally, sticky notes are easier to transfer to other displays, especially when getting rid of ideas or choosing the best ideas for the next stage of the ideate phase.

# Getting Unstuck

There will be times when students get stuck when trying to think of ideas for their solutions. They could need help focusing on a particular topic or issue related to their broad problem statement. Or, they could be focusing on the wrong problem, or their problem statement is too specific. There are two options that students can take to get unstuck:

**1.** Create subsidiary how-might-we (HMW) questions (see page 99) to ignite further brainstorming.

**2.** Reframe the problem statement to focus on a new aspect of the design challenge.

The first option involves students taking their problem statement and breaking it down into multiple smaller, HMW questions. Here is an example problem statement from the fourth-grade festival float project: People who've had exposure to the festival need a way to experience a festival float that will ignite wistful memories related to the festival from their past. From this statement, we can develop additional questions such as, "How might we provoke a gleeful emotion from the audience? How might we inspire our audience to celebrate the festival this year? How might we make a Carnival float that inspires people to give up something they love for 40 days?" These questions can help bring focus to a particular topic or issue, bring a unique perspective to the problem statement, and spark more spontaneous discussion and ideation. Developing good how-might-we questions can result in producing good ideas.

The second option in getting unstuck is for students to reframe the problem statement. This option is less likely to occur than the first but could be required if students are trying to solve the wrong problem. For example, in the Design Thinking Club, our students were given the following problem statement to solve: How can we organize the Performing Arts Center for the most efficient use of space while keeping like grades together? The students quickly realized that the real problem was not the seating arrangement, but the large amount of traffic caused by limited exit options in the auditorium. The question needed to be reframed so that the focus would be on how and where students could exit to decrease the amount of time it took to get to their classes. Since they were initially brainstorming for the wrong problem, the students were unable to come up with viable solutions.

Students can also have trouble generating ideas when their problem statement is too specific. In a fourth-grade engineering project, students designed solutions that would reduce the impact of natural disasters, such as tsunamis, landslides, volcanic eruptions, and earthquakes. During the define phase, some of the students developed problem statements that already contained an idea that they had in mind. Students have a natural tendency to think about solutions to the design challenge, even before defining the problem statement. For example, a student might write, "How might we block some of the waves to reduce the impact of the tsunami?" Instead the student could write, "How might we keep the people safe from the tsunami waves?" The latter question provides the student with a broader space to work with, allowing him or her to brainstorm different ways of answering the question (e.g., raising structures using open systems, blocking water with coastal dikes and levees, planting vegetation such as mangrove forests to block water, adding vertical evacuation levels in structures, etc.), whereas the first question limited the student to brainstorming different ways to block the water.

# Convergent Thinking: Choosing the Best Ideas

After accumulating a large quantity of ideas during the brainstorming session, students will start to analyze and evaluate their ideas, choosing the best ideas to move forward to the prototype phase. Through convergent thinking, students use their decision-making skills to choose multiple ideas that have the potential to bring drastic change, improvement, or resolution to the design challenge. Instead of going broad, this stage involves narrowing down to the best set of ideas for prototyping.

## How to Choose the Best Ideas

What entails the "best" ideas that students need to identify from their brainstorming work? The best ideas are the ones that have the most innovation potential, or the capacity to lead to and produce innovative solutions to the design challenge. Students can narrow down their ideas and choose the best ones for prototyping using a few helpful steps.

First, they should redirect the focus of their thinking back to the end user. Ask students, "Which ideas do you think would be the most valuable for your users? Which ones truly meet the needs and/or wants of your users?" These questions remind students that they are identifying ideas with their users in mind, and not based on their own preferences. There will be times when your students choose ideas based on what they want to do or create. Younger students especially like to add their own preferences into their ideas, which is not always the best for their end users.

Next, if students are unable to narrow down their ideas significantly, provide the option for them to vote for the best ideas by using the "potential" criteria. In *Design Thinking: Transforming Teams*, Bill Burnett describes how a team would silently vote for four ideas based on their potential and not their feasibility, two ideas that would *most likely succeed*, two ideas that would *most likely delight* end users, and two ideas that are the *most breakthrough*. For the last two criteria, most likely to delight and most breakthrough, the team would not have to consider any constraints. For my class, I've simplified the criteria for my students to the following:

- Most likely to make your user happy

- Most likely to work

- Most likely to be surprising/interesting for your user

After the team has voted for these three ideas, instruct students to combine them into one or two concrete solutions. Once the ideas are combined, students can start to create their blueprint for their prototype.

Blueprints help students transition into the prototype phase. For example, in the Apple device project, students synthesized their best ideas to create detailed drawings of their voice recorder, drawing the device in different viewpoints, identifying the dimensions and measurements of its parts, listing/labeling the materials needed to create the tangible object, and noting some constraints that might exist. The blueprints helped students to be focused and intentional during the prototype phase, switching their thinking from theoretical to tangible.

Before submitting their blueprints for approval, I ask students to check for four things:

**1.** How does it benefit their end user and/or solve the problem statement?

**2.** In their opinion, how is their solution *cool?*

**3.** Is the solution buildable?

**4.** How is the solution going to be tested so that it can elicit feedback and be improved?

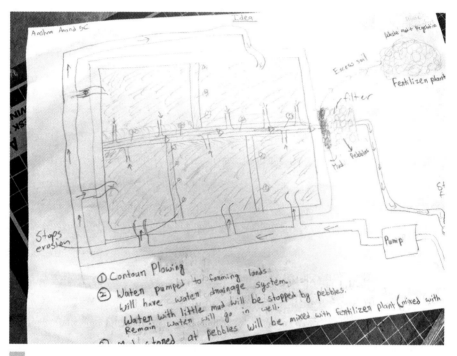

This is a fifth-grade student's blueprint of her farming system that prevents soil erosion and degradation by recycling any soil and water it uses.

We will discuss the last two questions in the next two chapters on the prototype and test phases. The first question, again, brings the focus back to the end user and the problem statement, making sure they understand without a doubt how their solution is the key to helping their end users.

For the second question, I use the word "cool" because it is an easy way to help my students understand that their solution should be innovative without actually saying the word "innovative," which can be a daunting and place unneeded pressure on the project. The word "cool" not only encompasses innovation, but can also mean something new, creative, different, special, unique, attractive, impressive, and/or interesting, but stated in a non-intimidating way. For the Apple device project, students had to identify how their voice recorder would be easy and intuitive to operate for English language learners, and how it would help them improve their English reading and speaking fluency.

Once they have answered these four questions, students may show you their blueprints for approval so that they can start creating their prototypes. The blueprint also contains information on how the prototype will be tested to see if it meets the success criteria. We will discuss this more in the next two chapters.

It is important to note that blueprints are not always going to be technical drawings for tangible objects. Solutions could come in the form of a strategic plan, an advertisement campaign, a website, a video, or anything that would help the end user. If students are planning to create this type of solution, then their blueprint would be a proposal of what their solution consists of. A video blueprint could include a storyboard, a list of video production equipment, and a list of materials for each scene. A website blueprint could include mockup sketches of each web page with layouts and types of media content. In the Design Thinking Club, my students created a blueprint for their assembly dismissal plan that included sketches of the different exit routes, possible seating areas for each class, procedural instructions, and how they planned to present their proposal to the administrators.

*Chapter Seven*

# Prototype Phase

The prototype phase is when students take their ideas and make them a reality, producing a prototype—an experimental model—that the end user can experience or possibly use to solve the problem statement. A prototype is a working model of combined ideas from the ideate phase, based on what students learned from the users. Created, altered, and in some cases, inspired by previous prototypes, this prototype will ultimately result in the final product.

During this phase, students have the opportunity to build, create, explore, experiment, and test assumptions as they keep their end users in mind. They will build their prototypes with a few critical goals:

**1.** Communicate clearly how their solutions will solve the problem statement.

**2.** Test, elicit feedback, identify new insights, and find unexpected failure points that can lead to improvements and refinements.

**3.** Provide opportunities to problem-solve and think through ideas that may arise through the act of making.

One of the most important things students should understand is not to get too attached to their prototypes. In this iterative phase, students may need to make drastic changes to their prototypes or even discard them completely. When facilitating this phase, teachers need to emphasize that the main purpose of these prototypes is for students to gain valuable feedback and surprising insights that could not be discovered without going through the prototyping and testing process.

A fifth-grade student created a motorized boat that captures plastic objects with its net. The student tested his remote-controlled boat in the school's swimming pool with Jeremy Jacobsen, our science specialist.

# Rapid Prototyping

Upon implementing my first DT project, I quickly found that the prototype and testing phases were extremely time-consuming. These initial DT projects did not include enough time for students to build and test their prototypes properly. However, with iterations on these projects, I improved in my ability to facilitate students during these phases, providing deadlines for when prototypes and tests needed to be completed, and ensuring that there was enough time for students to do so.

One method that helped students immensely was rapid prototyping, the process of quickly creating a prototype and then immediately gaining feedback from the end user or testing it out to find failure points that can later be improved. Our first graders used rapid prototyping to build their classmate a family activity tool. Once they created their prototype, they had the opportunity for their classmate to test out the tool. Students were able to gain additional insights and receive immediate feedback from their end user in a short period of time. With the information they gained, they went back to prototyping the next iteration of the family activity tool. Rapid prototyping is valuable because students are able to learn faster through the accelerated process of prototyping and testing.

During a brainstorming session, a second-grade student "thinks" with her hands, communicating her idea for a solution to erosion using colored pencils, a glue stick cap, and an eraser. This illustrates how integrated the DT phases are and how students jump to different phases without even being aware of it.

## Final Product vs. Low-Resolution Prototype

To show the benefits of rapid prototyping to your students, sketch out a scenario on the whiteboard where one student tries to create the final product in his first attempt, while a second student who uses the rapid prototyping method to create multiple iterations of low-resolution (low-res) prototypes. Let's say the first student spends three hours working on one prototype, trying to perfect every aspect of his creation, and trying to think about every error that could possibly occur if it was to be tested. Since he spends all his time building his one prototype, he only has time to test his prototype once right at the end of the three-hour session. He learns about one failure point but does not have time to make any changes to his prototype.

The second student, on the other hand, decides to use the rapid prototyping method and builds a low-res prototype that is constructed just enough for it to be tested within the first 10 minutes. **Low-res prototypes** are preliminary models made from basic materials built to gain information quickly and to speed up the progression of a design. She immediately tests her low-res prototype and finds a failure point. She jumps right back to the prototyping phase to fix the problem and then tests it again within 15 minutes. She goes through this iterative process for three hours, identifying numerous failure points and improving upon them to end up with a working prototype. At the end of my sketch demonstration, I ask my students which person in the scenario they believe would have created the better prototype.

Students gained a wealth of knowledge and feedback from the low-res prototypes they created in less than 10 minutes.

These prototypes are also great tools for students to communicate the ideas behind their solution to their team members, teachers/mentors, and end users for constructive feedback. For example, in the DT Club, my students visited Stacy Trinh to present three low-res prototypes of footstools that took them less than 10 minutes to create. They used small pieces of felt, cardboard, and pipe cleaners to construct miniature models that were about two to three inches tall. They understood that the models did not need to look perfect, but were only created to convey their ideas and gain feedback. The students explained the features of each footstool model, then Ms. Trinh identified the strengths of each model. The students used the additional information to start a new prototype that combined the strengths of each of the previous three models. By using low-res prototypes, the students were able to communicate their ideas to Ms. Trinh quickly so that they could learn insights and move onto better prototypes at an accelerated pace.

## Google Glass: Ideas for Rapid Prototyping

A great example of rapid prototyping that you can show your students is Google's development of Google Glass, a sleek, futuristic pair of glasses with an optical head-mounted display that allows users to operate apps through voice activation and has the capability to take photos and record video in an actual first-person point of view. This project was developed at Google's X company, where the mission is to invent and launch "moonshot" technologies to someday make the world a "radically better place." This is the same company that flies a network of balloons close to space to provide Internet for areas that do not get coverage, builds drones for delivery of goods and emergency medicine, and creates self-driving cars that have the potential to reduce road deaths caused by human error.

In his 2012 TEDYouth presentation, Tom Chi, the cofounder of X, shared with middle and high school students how his team developed the first versions of Google Glass using rapid prototyping to accelerate the innovation process. He shocks the audience by stating that it took them only one day to create a working version of the prototype glasses. It was the epitome of a low-res prototype using a netbook, projector, sheet protector, plexiglass, and coat hanger to simulate how the glasses could overlay digital content into the user's vision. In the next iteration of the prototype, the team decided to create an experience where the user could manipulate software with their hands. This prototype only took 45 minutes to make, again using basic materials such as a whiteboard, fishing line, hair bands, a binder clip, chopsticks, and a presentation clicker. This low-res prototype simulated how a person could use their hands to change the digital content on their glasses.

Chi provides three rules for rapid prototyping:

**1.** Find the quickest path to experience.

**2.** Doing is the best kind of thinking.

**3.** Use materials that move at the speed of thought to maximize your rate of learning.

By quickly creating a prototype, Chi's team was able to think through ideas by using their hands, create low-res prototypes as soon as they had an idea, and experience the prototypes to gain insights in a short period of time.

## Lowering the Resolution of Prototypes and Tests

During our Eco Trade Show (ETS) project (discussed on page 138), one student wanted to help people conserve water by designing a solution that would reduce the amount of time people take showers. His blueprint illustrated a shower system consisting of a digital timer that deactivates the water flow once the set time is up. If the average American used this solution and cut down their 20-minute showers to 10 minutes, they would save about 20 gallons of water per shower, or about 7,300 gallons per year. Even though his solution was creative and had great potential to reduce water consumption, he still needed to build and test this prototype. Since we did not have the materials and equipment to create it, we decided to lower the resolution of the proposed prototype but still maintain its ability to communicate the ideas behind his solution.

Through some discussion, we ended up with a low-res prototype with a mock-up timer display near the shower handles and a large container of water at the top. The bottom of the container had a tiny opening that represented the shower nozzle, which consistently trickled down small amounts of water. Through multiple tests, the student needed to figure out how much water it would take for it to all trickle down within a period of five minutes. Once he had the specific volume of water, he had created a low-res prototype that "shut down" the water flow after five minutes.

Another student wanted to create a system that would filter out particulate matter, such as soot, dust, debris, and ash, produced by greenhouse gas–emitting power plants. His blueprint contained a sketch of a power plant with smokestack filters that removed particulate matter from the smoke produced by the power plant. However, the initial testing plan for his prototype required him to burn different materials to create smoke. Since it would be dangerous for the student to conduct tests with fire in the classroom, he needed a way to transform his complex idea into a low-res prototype that could be tested without the risk of harming students and damaging the school. A visiting MIT student stopped by my classroom that day to help students with their blueprints. She suggested that this student could create a low-res prototype of the smokestack filter and test it by depositing debris and dust-like particles into it. The porous device would need to filter out all of the soot and debris for it to be successful. This low-res prototype and simplified test still conveyed his idea to reduce the amount of particulate matter that gets released by power plants into the air.

# Prototyping in Action: Fifth-Grade Eco Trade Show

## Driving Question

How will you, as an environmental engineer, design, build, and market a solution to an environmental issue?

## Summary

In the Eco Trade Show (ETS) project, our fifth-grade students spent a large portion of their time in the prototype and test phases. Students had to design a solution (manufactured product, strategic plan, media content, etc.) that would help reduce the impact of environmental problems caused by human activity. At the end of the unit, students presented their solutions at the Eco Trade Show where attendees took on the role of non-governmental organizations (NGO) who were there to invest in innovative solutions. The NGOs determined which solutions were the most effective in rehabilitating or preserving elements of a damaged environment.

## Classwork

In social studies, students learned about basic economic concepts to prepare them for the Eco Trade Show, such as understanding goods and services, the currency system, supply and demand, the needs and wants of investors (NGOs), and the differences between cost, profit, and revenue. In writing, students used their persuasive writing skills to help market their solution at the trade show. Our science specialists, Elizabeth DiRenzo and Jeremy Jacobsen, developed activities to help students understand the Earth's major spheres (geosphere, atmosphere, biosphere, and hydrosphere), interacting systems that can affect environments and their processes. They also experienced firsthand how water was rehabilitated at the local water-treatment center. Using what they learned in multiple disciplines, students used the design process to create a solution that they presented at the Eco Trade Show.

## Diverse Range of Prototypes

In past ETS projects, students created biodegradable bioplastic to replace petroleum-based plastics used for everyday items, portable solar cookers to reduce the use of nonrenewable resources for heating, a vermicompost home kit that decomposes food waste to create fertilizer for backyard gardens, and a dew water collector for regions with frequent droughts. Not all the solutions students designed were tangible objects. Students also created the likes of a website to bring awareness to an environmental issue and educate people on how they can help, a proposal that would reduce the amount of land grabbing (the leasing of large areas of land by foreign governments and companies that negatively affects the native people in those areas) in different parts of Africa, and an app that allows users to organize carpools quickly to reduce greenhouse gas emissions.

This fifth-grade student designed a solution where the greenhouse gases produced by the Korean BBQ restaurant are filtered and transferred to an adjacent greenhouse. The crops in the greenhouse use the CO2 and are grown to be served in the restaurant. This student's filtration system prototype is shown on the right.

In most DT projects, students get to decide on the solution they want to design, creating a personalized learning environment where they choose what and how they learn. Providing choice will result in a diverse range of solutions to facilitate and assess.

## More Fifth-Grade ETS Solutions

**1.** Solar-powered boat that captures floating plastic in the ocean

**2.** System that filters garbage pollution for urban runoff with the capability of easy garbage removal

**3.** Toilet system where water used from the sink is transferred to the toilet to be reused.

**4.** Car tunnel that incorporates trees to remove $CO_2$ inside the tunnel, and includes a rainwater irrigation system and solar powered artificial lighting.

**5.** Tram system that is powered by the steam created by the water being heated by geothermal energy

**6.** Farming system that reuses water, prevents erosion, and does not use pesticide for its crops

**7.** Product that limits the movement of faucet handles to reduce the amount of waterflow

In the ETS project, students were able to choose from a diverse selection of environmental problems, and through the DT process, they developed their own unique testing plans to see if their prototypes were successful. Their blueprints included a plan for prototype testing so that they could identify failure points and see how well they met the criteria for success. This part of the blueprint can be the most challenging for students.

In an average design or engineering project, students carry out the same fair tests with controlled variables, usually planned out by the teacher.

However, in this project, each test needed to be designed specifically for the environmental issue that the student chose. This required students to be creative in how they tested their prototypes; many students needed help from teachers to come up with tests because of the complexity of their environmental problem. If a student is unable to create a testing plan because of the complexity of his or her design problem and prototype, then the student and the teacher can collaboratively work on lowering the "resolution" of the prototype and develop a simplified testing plan.

# Facilitation and Mentorship

Complex projects can be challenging for both students and teachers because of the rigor and continuous inquiry they require. For that reason, it is important for a number of passionate educators from different disciplinary backgrounds to facilitate students throughout the DT process, especially in the prototype and testing phases.

Larry Rosenstock, CEO of High Tech High, one of the most innovative and reputable schools in the US, defines rigor as "being in the company of a passionate adult who is rigorously pursuing inquiry in the area of their subject matter and is inviting students along as peers in that adult discourse." These passionate adults model the DT mindsets and practices, and encourage, guide, and support students to think critically and creatively to solve or improve these complex, real-world problems and experiences.

In the ETS project, at least two to three teachers were present for every class during the prototyping and testing phases to ensure that every student would have the opportunity to work with and gain advice from an experienced and knowledgeable adult. Both the teachers and students learned from the partnership as they went through the phases of the DT process. Additionally, the fifth-grade homeroom teachers scheduled some of the neighboring high school teachers and their students to come to the class to provide further mentorship. The high school students were also informed of the collaborative plussing technique to ensure that their role was to facilitate, build upon and improve ideas, and provide constructive feedback. At one point we had six teachers and a whole high school class in the classroom helping out our fifth-grade students prototype and test.

Gene MacLachlan and a class of high school students provided additional feedback and facilitation for our fifth-grade students who were working on their solutions to their environmental problem..

So, how do you know if you, your colleagues, and visiting mentors are effective facilitators? According to Larry Rosenstock, this depends on the sophistication of your students' work. "If your kids are producing work that's worth doing and that has a lasting value and learning that's worth learning, you're a good teacher," Rosenstock says. In our latest iteration of the project, I found this to be true; compared to the first year we implemented this project, I have found that students are generating more innovative solutions to their problem statements. As we gained more experience as facilitators, we improved in assisting students in transforming their creative ideas into innovative realities, guiding them to think critically, creatively, and to go beyond the obvious.

Personally, I believe I've improved as a design facilitator by attempting to emulate the work of David Wallace, a professor at MIT's Mechanical Engineering program. Wallace teaches the famed 2.009: Product Engineering Processes capstone course, where students apply what they've learned as an undergraduate to design and build a market-ready product. At the end of the course, teams of 15 to 20 students present their final products to a live audience of more than a thousand people, which includes various academics, product designers, and entrepreneurs. A huge part of the popularity and success of the course is due to the work and teaching style of David Wallace.

In a tribute video celebrating Wallace's 20 years of teaching this course, his students and colleagues shared some of the qualities and characteristics that make him such a great educator of design. They described him as enthusiastic, passionate, empowering, and open-minded, someone who is willing to spend the extra hours to not only help students improve their products, but also improve their learning experience in the course. These are the same qualities that I believe are needed for teachers who are facilitating students in the DT process.

# Makerspace, Tools, and Materials

The majority of the work done in the prototyping and testing phases for my DT projects have occurred in a classroom **makerspace**, where students have the ability to manufacture products using different tools, materials, and technologies. Two types of DT projects are completed in my makerspace.

The first type require specific materials, tools, and technologies. For example, fourth-grade students used microcontrollers to program electrical components to perform simple tasks for their mechanical float models. They also learned to use precision knives to cut and score foam board for the casing of their Apple voice recorder. Fifth-grade students learned to use hand tools and fasteners to construct their Breakout EDU boxes. Even the second-grade students learned to use box cutters to cut and fold foam board. It is your responsibility to teach your students safety rules and train them to use the tools that are specifically required for your DT projects.

The elementary makerspace provides students with the tools, supplies, and technologies needed to manufacture their products.

The second type of DT projects done in the makerspace are those that allow students to use any type of materials to create their prototypes. The makerspace consists of recyclables (plastics, cardboard, etc.), electronic components (LEDs, wires, solar panels, motors, etc.), woodworking materials (wood, dowels, sandpaper, hand tools, fasteners, etc.), and other consumables (foam board, duct tape, wood craft sticks, paper cups, etc.). Depending on what solution students want to create for their problem statement, they can ask permission to use any of the materials and tools available to build their prototype. For example, in the ETS project, students identified specific materials and tools in their blueprint needed to create their solution for their environmental issue.

Although we are fortunate to have a makerspace, by no means is one required to implement a DT project. You can have your own makerspace in your classroom by furnishing a section of the room with low-cost consumables (straws, wood craft sticks, masking tape, construction paper, etc.), recyclables, and basic craft school supplies. Even a storage cart furnished with these low-tech materials would be beneficial for students in the prototype phase. The majority of our DT projects only required these low-cost, low-tech materials and tools.

Additionally, the workspace, tools, and materials are not the most important aspects of a makerspace. It is the maker mindset and culture that propel students to produce creative and inventive products. The classroom environment should encourage students to explore with their hands, experiment, work collaboratively, learn from failure, and think positively. Your makerspace can be a place where students develop grit, a growth mindset, and initiative.

*Chapter Eight*

# Test Phase

As stated earlier, the testing phase allows students to gain feedback and insights that may not be possible without testing their prototypes. Through these tests, students will be able to identify aspects of their prototype that did not work well or that the end user did not find functional or pleasing. These "failures" give students the opportunity to fix and improve aspects of their prototypes. In our class, we celebrate failures during our tests because we understand that failures allow us to learn and improve.

However, failing can be difficult to accept for most students. It results in the same feelings we get when we get stuck during our brainstorming sessions. Not only does it make us feel uncomfortable and insecure, failing can also be embarrassing, painful, and annoying; some students even feel anger. Despite this, I have observed my students overcome their fear of failure and embrace it as a learning opportunity. Failure is part of the culture in my classroom. Give students permission to be different, try new things, and innovate, even if this means pursuing the unconventional.

# Embracing Failure

There are a few ways to help your students embrace failure. First, show them that teachers fail all the time. I provide examples of how I failed at numerous things in my life, telling students about my chaotic student-teaching experiences when I had no behavioral management skills, how I forgot my lines when I presented a conference talk on stage in front of 350 of my colleagues, and some of the horrible projects I developed and implemented in my first year as STEM coordinator. Second, show students some examples of successful people who have failed countless times. Describe how their failures taught them lifelong lessons that helped them to succeed in their future endeavors.

Michael Jordan, an NBA Hall-of-Fame player who is famous for performing phenomenally under pressure, attempted and missed 26 career game-winning shots.

Walt Disney was fired from the *Kansas City Star* newspaper because he "lacked imagination and had no good ideas."

In 1985, Steve Job was fired from Apple, the company he cofounded, but returned in 1996 to make it one of the most valuable companies in the world.

In his commencement address at Stanford University, Steve Jobs stated how devastating it was for him to leave the company he started. However, through his failures, he learned a valuable lesson. "I didn't see it then, but it turned out that getting fired from Apple was the best thing that could have ever happened to me," he said. "The heaviness of being successful was replaced by the lightness of being a beginner again, less sure about everything. It freed me to enter one of the most creative periods of my life." The heartbreaking experience forced him to return to a beginner's mindset, enhancing his ability to be creative and try innovative things. Through examples and quotes like these, students learn that failure is part of the journey to success and they are not the only ones who encounter failure.

Another way to help students embrace failure is to show examples of how their peers are learning from failures. When I observe a great example of a student learning from failure, I ask for the attention of the class and describe how the person used what they learned from a failed test to improve his or her prototype. Providing peer examples brings clarity to the idea of failure being a learning tool, making the abstract idea of learning from failure more tangible and motivating students to move past their initial reactions to failure and use what was learned to create a more successful prototype.

# Testing with End Users

When students test with end users, it is another chance for them to empathize and learn something new that could be used to refine their current prototypes. Testing brings the focus back to the end user to reveal hidden insights that the students would have never foreseen without the end user experiencing their prototype. According to the d.school, there are four aspects that students need to consider when testing with end users: (1) the prototype, (2) context and scenario, (3) the interaction between the user and designer, and (4) the process and method used to observe, capture feedback, and reflect.

Let's look back at the second-grade project where students designed a nature-inspired toy for their kindergarten peers. We wanted our second-grade students to test their toy prototypes in an authentic scenario where their end users would actually play with the toys. We thought it would be most appropriate if the kindergartners experienced the toy prototypes during their free-choice period, the only time they get to play with actual toys and games. After being paired up with a kindergartner, the second graders explained the context of the toy test briefly, just enough so that the user knew what to do. By not being explaining things in detail, the kindergartners had the opportunity to explore through hands-on play while the toy designers got to observe what aspects of their design did not work, was difficult to use, or was being used the wrong way. Once the testing was done, they took their findings and went back to the makerspace to make improvements on their toy prototype.

Before the testing session, it was important to prepare both parties for their interaction so that they proceeded in the right testing mindset. We prompted the toy designers to start focusing their attention on the aspects of their prototypes that needed to be improved during the testing phase; this was a very different focus compared to the prototype phase where students were constantly thinking about how to make their prototype successful.

The testing phase requires students to not get defensive about the feedback they receive about their prototype or justify the reasoning behind their design, but instead, to be attentive to feedback and surprising insights. We reminded kindergartners that their participation in testing the toys was crucial to the improvement and success of their older peers; their role was to provide constructive feedback, building upon the ideas that they experienced, and provide suggestions or alternatives to aspects that might need to be improved.

The students captured their observational findings and user feedback through a simple tool called the Feedback Capture Grid. Students divided a sheet of paper into four quadrants. In the first quadrant, they wrote down their users' feedback on what they liked about the toy prototype. The second quadrant contained the users' constructive feedback, while the third quadrant contained the questions that arose during the testing. The fourth quadrant contained new ideas or improvements that emerged from the tests. This feedback tool helped students be more intentional in what they were observing and the information they were looking to record. Using what they compiled in their Feedback Capture Grid, they proceeded back to the prototype phase to refine and improve their toy prototypes.

A second-grade student improved her toy design by using the feedback she gained from her end users during the testing phase. In the photo, you can see the Feedback Capture Grid with its four quadrants.

## Four Aspects of Testing: Examples

|  | Fifth-Grade Breakout EDU | Design Thinking Club | First-Grade Family Activity Tool |
|---|---|---|---|
| Prototype | Breakout EDU Game | Desk organizer | Tool that would enhance the experience of a classmate's family activity |
| Context and Scenario | Playing the game in the classroom | Mr. Persaud's office | Imagining the use of the tool in the setting of the family activity |
| User Interaction | Designer facilitates the game and observes user experience | Student interviews with end users | Students observe users, look for insights, and listen to feedback |
| Capturing Observations and Feedback | Players add feedback by posting sticky notes onto the boxes | Students listen for feedback | Verbal constructive feedback |

# Testing without End Users

In the third-grade Schoolhouse Design project (page 92), students had to design a schoolhouse for children in specific regions around the world. Through research, students empathized with the region's people and their culture, as well as learned about the weather-related hazards (WRH) that occur in the region. However, this project did not provide students with actual end users that they interacted with and gained feedback from. In the future, we hope to connect our students with keypals from each of the regions to take on the role as end users. This year, since they did not have any end users to test with, we had students test their schoolhouse designs against weather-related hazard simulations in testing stations.

While it is preferable to have end users interact with prototypes for feedback, for projects where end users are unavailable, it is still beneficial to have students go through the testing phase by providing them with another way to test their prototypes.

For regions with WRHs that are characterized with high winds, I used a leaf blower to blast air toward the Schoolhouse Design prototypes to see if they remained standing. For regions with hurricanes, students tested their designs by pouring multiple cups of water through a strainer to simulate heavy rain and high water levels. Other students tested their designs with a heat lamp to simulate regions with heat waves. These students checked whether or not the temperature inside their schoolhouse was cooler than it was outside of it. In regions with droughts, students also tested their schoolhouses' ability to capture and store water in the extremely rare circumstances it rained. We also tested blizzard-resistant prototypes by placing them in the freezer of the teachers' lounge to see whether or not the temperature inside the prototype was far warmer than the temperature of the freezer. Finally, for regions with flash floods, students pushed large amounts of water toward their prototype within a large plastic container.

With an alternative testing opportunity, students still got to learn about and experience the testing process. The testing process also provides students with the opportunity to rapid prototype, fail, learn from mistakes, and make improvements while developing their grit and the ability to be more persistent.

A student tests her schoolhouse prototype with a thermometer and a heat lamp to see if it would be an effective solution for schoolchildren in regions with heat waves. She included a solar-powered fan inside the prototype to cool down the interior of the schoolhouse.

Schoolhouse prototype with stilts and an additional structural level for vertical evacuation to withstand flash floods and help keep schoolchildren safe.

# Iteration

Iteration in DT is the act of repeating a particular action or process to produce a better outcome. I've discussed the iterative nature of the prototype and testing phases, describing how students repeat the prototyping and test process to improve their solutions. Iteration can take place in the other phases of DT process as well. Students might need to develop multiple iterations of a problem statement to bring to light the true problem they need to work on, perform iterations of brainstorming sessions with various topics to generate a viable set of solutions for prototyping, or iterate empathy work to gain more meaningful insights that will help them with their design.

What is most beautiful about the iteration element of DT is that it shows students how learning, designing, and solving problems can take place in a nonlinear way. With iteration, actions are repeated based on a given need. If students need to learn more about the end user or the problem, they can jump to the empathize phase and perform more empathy work. If students are unable to create working prototypes, they can go back to the ideate phase and generate more ideas for possible solutions.

This concept also teaches students that learning involves trial and error. They don't need to get it right, understand the content, or perform a skill correctly the first time. It liberates them from feeling like they have to be perfect, encouraging them to be creative and act on their instincts. Additionally, students gradually gain self-confidence and courage by fixing their mistakes, improving their work, and overcoming their failures through iteration. They slowly start to trust their own abilities and judgment to solve problems creatively.

# Part Three

# Design Thinking in the Classroom

*Chapter Nine*

# Pedagogy

My goal in education has been to empower as many students as possible. I quickly learned that I could empower students by providing them with authentic scenarios and experiences in my classroom, and equipping them with the real-world skills needed to be successful in future endeavors. You, too, can be a designer, empowering your students with a design framework that simulates the real world in your classroom.

## The ACT Project

In February of 2016, I was invited to attend the Google Innovator Academy at Google's Headquarters in Mountain View, California. For two days, our cohort of educators learned about innovative approaches to teaching and learning. We also got to start on a project that would have the potential to transform an aspect of education in a positive way.

I decided to join forces with two fellow Google innovators, Jessica Loucks and David Hotler, to develop a design framework that would eventually be known as The ACT Project. It is a holistic design framework focused around simulating and directly utilizing the behaviors, strategies, and practices found in successful learning environments to transform students into empowered citizens. Empowered citizens are individuals who have the knowledge, skills, dispositions, and learning abilities to succeed in their future professions, projects, personal lives, and civic duties. They are future-ready individuals who can learn and complete tasks no matter the situation or circumstance; they are able to learn continuously in a world of constant change and innovation.

ACT stands for the three foundational pillars of the design framework: (1) Applied Learning Practices, (2) Culture of Hope, and (3) Transdisciplinary Pedagogy. Applied learning practices are learning methods students use to complete rigorous challenges and develop innovative solutions to complex problems. The second pillar, Culture of Hope, is composed of social norms, attitudes, and dispositions that nurture successful, real-world learning. Finally, transdisciplinary pedagogies are teaching approaches and methods that provide students with authentic, real-world challenges that require knowledge and skills from multiple disciplines. These three pillars work together and depend on one another to achieve the goal of developing empowered citizens.

The DT process is an example of an applied learning practice because it's a method for creative problem-solving. Implementing DT into the classroom also ensures a culture of hope because it promotes and supports learning-friendly attitudes and dispositions, such as growth mindset, practical optimism, action-oriented thinking, and grit, that encourage and support real-world learning. However, DT does not account for transdisciplinary pedagogy. DT in the classroom needs to be accompanied by transdisciplinary pedagogy since DT involves authentic experiences and real-world context. Without this type of pedagogy, DT cannot be implemented effectively.

## Transdisciplinary Pedagogy

Transdisciplinary pedagogy involves the teaching approaches and methods that simulate the learning and work done in real-world scenarios. This type of pedagogy requires students to rigorously apply knowledge and skills from multiple disciplines to solve authentic, real-world challenges and answer authentic, meaningful questions.

Many of the projects and tasks we do as adults involve the skills and knowledge of multiple subject areas, and require meaningful, hands-on, inquiry-based learning. So why don't we provide our students the same type of projects and tasks? Schools have created artificial barriers between subject areas that are taught in isolation, but actually overlap naturally. Our obsession with classifying knowledge and skills into categories can result in artificial learning, not relevant to what students need to thrive in the future. Transdisciplinary pedagogy breaks down these barriers and provides real-world context through real-world enterprises that require stakeholders to take on the role of professionals

# Project-Based Learning: Bringing the Real World to the Classroom

The transdisciplinary pedagogy we use to help implement DT into the classroom is project-based learning (PBL). It provides our teachers with a method of developing projects that are designed in a way that is true to what happens in real life, especially in professional realms. These projects provide the learning structure and real-world context needed for students to utilize the DT process productively. A lot of the PBL resources we use are from the Buck Institute for Education (BIE), a nonprofit organization and leader in providing professional development for educators on how to use the teaching approach. One of the resources I've relied heavily on is the BIE's book, *PBL in the Elementary Grades* by Sara Hallermann and John Larmer. According to the book, PBL consists of "a meaningful question to explore, an engaging real-world problem to solve, or a challenge to design or create something," a need to "inquire into the topic by asking questions and developing their own answers," and finally collaboratively work to "create high-quality products and present their work to other people."

This book is a great resource for planning assessments and learning tasks in PBL, and for strategies on how to manage PBL projects effectively, such as developing classroom culture, guiding inquiry, and teaching critical thinking. PBL is a powerful pedagogical tool that enhances the DT experience with its emphasis on real-world problems, inquiry, and collaboration. Since DT is most useful in these real-world contexts, not providing the same type of context in the classroom makes the use of the DT process superficial.

## BIE's Essential Project Design Elements

- Key Knowledge, Understandings, and Success Skills
- Challenging Problem or Question
- Sustained Inquiry
- Authenticity
- Student Voice and Choice
- Reflection
- Critique and Revision
- Public Product

# PBL Project

In PBL, there are four stages in the sequencing of a project: (1) Launch project: Entry event and driving question, (2) Build knowledge and skills to answer the driving question, (3) Develop and revise products that answer the driving question, and (4) Present products that answer the driving question. These four stages consist of eight essential elements of PBL project design, highlighted below in bold text.

In the first stage, the students experience an entry event that captures their interest about the general topic of the project. The teacher then introduces the driving question (DQ), a **challenging problem or question** that communicates the purpose of the project, sparks the interest of the students, and provides real-world context to bring **authenticity** to the students' work. In the second stage, students gain **key knowledge, understandings, and success skills** from multiple disciplines that are required to answer the DQ through **sustained inquiry** and engaging in meaningful lessons and activities. In the next stage, students are given **voice** (make their own decisions) and **choice** (select how they work and what to create) when developing their products for the DQ. This stage includes opportunities for the **critique and revision** of their products. Finally, in the last stage, students present their **public products** to an authentic audience to demonstrate their mastery of the project's learning goals, and then **reflect** on their learning and their effectiveness to answer the DQ. The section below shows how the DT process fits well into the flow of a PBL project.

## Interrelationship Between BIE's Flow of PBL Project and the DT Process

**1.** Launch Project: Entry Event & Driving Question

Students are introduced to the driving question, which would contain information about the design problem or experience and the end users they will be designing for.

**2.** Build Knowledge and Skills to Answer DQ

Students engage in inquiry and empathy work to gain the knowledge and skills needed to answer the driving question (empathy phase).

Students define a problem statement that includes the insights they gained through inquiry and empathy work (define phase).

**3.** Develop and Revise Products that Answer DQ

Students brainstorm solutions (ideate phase), build prototypes (prototype phase), test with end users (test phase), and revise and improve prototypes (iteration) based on the test results and feedback given.

**4.** Present Products that Answer DQ

Students present their final product to the end user to solve their problem or improve their experience in a particular scenario.

# Chapter Ten

# Creating DT Projects

One of the most important things you need to know when designing, planning, and implementing your first DT project is that it is not going to go exactly as you plan. Think of it as if you were testing your first prototype. It won't be exactly what you envision, but it will reveal unexpected learnings and identify possible improvements that will benefit the experience of your users, the students, in the next iteration of the project. Don't be intimidated by the uncertainty; instead, embrace it and be experimental because you might end up with an amazing DT project or begin the process of producing something great.

Additionally, don't put too much pressure on yourself to create a DT project that incorporates all of the phases. For your first DT project, focus on one phase and try to do it well. With the next iterations of the project, add more meaningful learning activities that will enhance the learning experiences of the other phases. A lot of the projects that are introduced in this book have phases that are weaker than others. Designing DT projects is an iterative process.

Lastly, even though this book showcases DT projects for elementary grades, the process can still be applied to middle and high school settings.

# Single-Subject Approach

There are two paths that you can take in designing a DT project. The first is the **single-subject approach** where you identify one or more standards from a particular subject area and brainstorm ways of using them to create a DT challenge that contains a real-world scenario. This is by far my favorite part of designing a DT project. You get to be creative and design a project that is as engaging, meaningful, and authentic as you want it to be—a project that you wish you could have worked on when you were your students' age.

## Process of Designing DT Project

1. Identify content standards or learning goals that you want your students to demonstrate mastery in.

2. Brainstorm real-world scenarios that would incorporate these standards with the DT method.

3. Identify one real-world scenario that would best incorporate these standards and the DT method in a relevant, meaningful, and engaging way.

4. Identify the end user(s) of the project who will benefit from your students' work.

5. Develop a driving question that encompasses the DT project, and drives student exploration and inquiry.

One of the most important tasks of designing a DT project will be to identify the end users who will benefit from your students' real-world solution. Who will your students empathize with? Who will use or experience the solution they design? Ideally, students will be able to interact with end users and perform empathy work. However, end users are not always accessible during a project (Schoolhouse Design, page 92). If this is the case, I recommend still implementing the project even if the end users are theoretical. It is still valuable to have students try to put themselves in their end users' shoes and gain empathy of their needs through research. This is given the fact that implementing these projects is iterative as well. You will have another chance next year to provide real end users that students can interact and partner up with.

# Transdisciplinary Approach

The second path, the **transdisciplinary approach,** is where a teacher or a group of teachers attempt to integrate the content standards of multiple subject areas to create one DT project that includes end users. Initially, I look at the content standards of each subject area, the expectations of what students will achieve. Most of the academic standards I used group their grade-specific learning goals into topics. For example, the Next Generation Science Standards (NGSS) combine their associated standards into "topic arrangements." An example of an NGSS topic arrangement in kindergarten is Forces and Interactions: Pushes and Pulls, which consists of learning goals that describe how students should be able to investigate the effects of pushes and pulls in different strengths or different directions on an object's motion, and find out if a design is able to change the speed or direction of an object by a push or a pull. These groupings made it easier for us to see which standards worked well together to create a real-world project that focused on specific end users. If you or your team cannot find connections between the standards of multiple disciplines, try unpacking the standards into knowledge and skills, and see if any of them could be integrated.

Use this chart to create and document a DT project:

## Creating a Design Thinking Project

| | Subjects | | | | | |
|---|---|---|---|---|---|---|
| **Desired Results** | List standards or learning goals | | | | | |
| **Project Summary** | Real-world scenario | | | | | |
| | End user | | | | | |
| | Empathy work | | | | | |
| | Driving question | | | | | |
| | Final product | | | | | |

Let's take a look again at the second-grade City Plan project (page 73). We first examined all the topics of the second-grade science, social studies, engineering, writing, and technology standards to find which standards could have the potential to be used for one project. This step requires teachers to be creative and use their critical thinking skills to see how the standards or learning goals can work together; it is similar to assembling pieces to a perplexing puzzle that don't seem to fit with one another or combine to create a new entity.

Since we felt that skill subjects, where students learn fundamental skills like reading, writing, and information technology, are easier areas to integrate and are involved in most real-world scenarios, we decided to first look at content subjects, like mathematics, science, and social studies, to see if there were any less obvious real-world connections.

We found that in social studies, students needed to learn how a community meets the needs of its citizens and understand specific mapping concepts that show the features and landforms of an area. In science, we found that students needed to learn about the processes that shape the Earth slowly or quickly through water and wind. From these standards, we brainstormed design challenge ideas that contained real-world scenarios. We asked, "What type of solution or end product will the users be able to use or experience to help them solve their problem or improve their experiences?" We finally came up with the concept of having students learn about the needs of the local community members to develop a city plan that incorporated a map of the community, its landforms, and its bodies of water using the DT process.

| | Standards or Learning Goals |
|---|---|
| Engineering | Engineering process: Ask questions, make observations, and gather information; define a simple problem; develop a simple sketch, drawing, or physical model; analyze data from tests of two objects. |
| Science | Changing landforms: Changes on Earth can occur quickly or slowly; slow or prevent wind or water from changing the land; land and bodies of water |
| Social studies | Community meeting the needs of citizens: Identify and explain how communities meet the needs of their citizens |
| Writing | Persuasive letter writing: Strategies for persuasive writing, express stance and logical reasoning and sequence |
| Technology | Creative communication: Communicate complex ideas clearly and effectively by creating or using a variety of digital objects; publish or present content that customizes the message and medium. |
| Design | Design thinking: Empathy, Define, Ideate, Prototype, Test, Iterate |

**Real-world scenario:** Second grade will create a city plan that will help improve the school's local community.

**End users:** Community members, specifically residents and businesses.

**Empathy work:** Interview residents and businesses and visit community to make observations.

The transdisciplinary path can get complicated and difficult because of the numerous moving parts of the project. It requires the collaboration of multiple teachers with weekly meetings that assure everyone is on the same page. A transdisciplinary DT project reminds me of a mechanical watch with intricate gears and parts working together to make the device work properly. Students will work on one part of the project in one class, and another part in a different class, which creates a learning phenomena where the success of lessons in science might be determined by what is going on in social studies.

It can be daunting to have to analyze numerous standards from multiple subject areas. I recommend involving the curriculum coordinator in this process if one is available at your school. This path also requires buy-in from teachers, administrators, elective teachers, and student-support specialists.

# Develop a Driving Question

After identifying the project's design challenge, the end users, and the final product that the students will produce, it is time to develop a driving question (DQ) that encompasses the design challenge and guides students throughout the project. This DQ would be introduced at the beginning of the project, after the entry event. In our City Plan example (page 73), the DQ was the following: "How can we as urban planners design a city plan that improves the local community?" From this question, students would be able to identify the design challenge, the end users, and the type of product they will be designing.

The DQ can also be broken down into subsidiary questions in each subject area. This allows students to work on the same project but in different classrooms. The students would ask themselves, "What do we need to know in the subject area to answer the driving question?" In social studies, students could ask, "What is the purpose of a city plan and what does it include?" or "How do we improve a community?" In science, students could ask, "How could landforms and bodies of water affect the community?"

To develop our DQs, we use the BIE tool called the Driving Question Tubric 2.0. The tool is called a "tubric" because it is a "tube" that contains different slots that you can adjust. The structure of the question is broken down into four parts: framing words, person or entity, action or challenge, and audience or purpose. The tool gives teachers choices for each of these parts to produce a DQ based on the project that they came up with.

## Driving Question Tubric 2.0

| Framing Words | Person or Entity | Action or Challenge | Audience or Purpose |
|---|---|---|---|
| How can... | I<br>We | Build...<br>Create...<br>Make... | Real-World Problem |
| How do... | We as,<br>[Roles]<br>[Occupations] | Design...<br>Plan... | For a Public Audience |
| Should... | [Town]<br>[City]<br>[County] | Solve... | For a School |
| Could... | [State]<br>[Nation] | Write... | For a Classroom |
| What... | [Community]<br>[Organization] | Propose...<br>Decide... | For an Online Audience |

Here is the DQ of the second-grade City Plan project divided into the four parts: "How can (framing words) we as urban planners (person or entity), design (action or challenge) a city plan that improves the local community (audience or purpose)?" For most of our DT projects, we had students take on the role of professionals (person) who design (action) a solution to a real-world problem (purpose). Again, it is crucial to distinguish the difference between the DQ that the teachers introduce at the beginning of the project and the problem statement that students formulate in the define phase. The DQ describes the design challenge or the real-world problem that the students will be working on, whereas the problem statement, formulated later in the define phase, describes the specific needs of the end users and the insights gained during the empathy work.

**Driving Question:** "How can we as urban planners design a city plan that improves the local community?"

**Problem Statement:** Business people and students (users) need a way to rest and relax (need) because, surprisingly, they work or study for eight to nine hours each day (insight).

We then integrated NGSS engineering standards by having students develop and test solutions that would reduce the impact of erosion on the community since it sits on the side of a hill. Students made observations and gathered information about the possible erosion that could occur in the community, developed multiple sketches of erosion solutions, and analyzed data from testing their erosion solutions. From there, we started to add the skill subjects into the project and determined what type of product students would create in each of these skill subjects. We decided that students would write a persuasive letter to a civil engineer to explain how the city plan would meet the needs of the community members (writing) and create a video campaign that showcases their ideas to bring positive change to the community (technology).

## Final Products

| Subject | Standard or Learning Goal | Final Product |
|---|---|---|
| Engineering | Engineering process | Erosion solutions for community on the hill |
| Science | Changing landforms | Landform landscape model |
| Social studies | Meeting the needs of citizens | City plan |
| Writing | Persuasive letter writing | Persuasive letter to civil engineer for city plan |
| Technology | Creative communication | Video campaign for community |
| Design | Design thinking | City plan |

Since we used standards to develop our DT project, we can use the final products of the project to assess what students have learned and are able to do. The products become the assessment tools to see if their learning goals were met. For example, the social studies teacher can use the city plan to determine whether or not they understand that the community meets the needs of its citizens, and whether students are able to use mapping concepts to depict the community and its geographic features. The engineering teacher can use the erosion solutions to assess if students are able to prototype solutions that reduce the impact of Earth processes (erosion) in the community. These products/assessments will need evaluation criteria to determine how well students meet the learning goals.

# Planning DT Curriculum, Assessments, and Instruction

The Understanding by Design (UbD) framework has been a valuable tool for me in planning for DT curriculum, assessments, and instruction. This framework provides a backward design process where the curriculum is developed by first identifying the desired results. The three stages of UbD are:

**Stage 1:** Identify Desired Results

**Stage 2:** Determine Assessment Evidence

**Stage 3:** Plan Learning Experiences and Instruction

## Desired Results

In the first stage, Identify Desired Results, teachers examine the content standards and identify performance goals that they want their students "to do with what they have learned."

When I first started teaching my design class, I looked online to find design thinking standards that I could use to guide me in developing DT curriculum and assessments. To my surprise, I was unable to find any standards that were specifically for design thinking. I decided to use Engineering Design standards from the Next Generation Science

Standards (NGSS) because the content standards were being used in the science class, and the engineering process was similar to the design process. I altered some of the terminology to make it fit better for our DT projects. However, the differences between the two processes were too difficult to ignore; therefore, the design standards from the International Society for Technology (ISTE) standards were added. Finding myself frustrated with using a miscellaneous assortment of standards, I decided to develop my own standards over the summer that would be specifically developed for design thinking in education.

The Design Thinking Standards (DTS) provide educators with a foundation of what students are expected to learn and do when using the design thinking method. The standards were inspired by the work and teachings of the d.school and the K12 Lab Network. I use these standards to establish what my students will be able to do, know, and understand when utilizing the DT process (Appendix, page 180).

## Evidence

In the second stage of UbD, teachers determine the assessments that will provide evidence of student understanding and their ability to achieve the desired results. Assessments can be performance tasks where students "apply their learning to a new and authentic situation" or other evidences such as "traditional quizzes, tests, observations, and work samples." According to Jay McTighe, the lead of ISTE's UbD team, performance tasks allow students to apply knowledge and skills, are open-ended, provide authentic contexts, and integrate multiple subject areas and twenty-first century skills.

The majority of the assessments I give for the DT projects are performance tasks because of the action-oriented, real-world nature of DT. These DT projects require students to apply knowledge and skills from multiple subjects, and offer the opportunity to use creative practices to produce a diverse range of ideas and prototypes. Students were assessed on their ability to gain valuable information through empathy work, develop actionable problem statements that contain needs and insights, brainstorm multiple, creative solutions, create prototypes end users can engage and interact with, and test prototypes to solicit feedback, identify failure points, and use new learnings to create the next iterations of prototypes.

## Learning Plan

Finally, in the last stage of the UbD planning process, the learning plan, teachers plan out the activities for each DT phase, the sequencing of these activities, and the required resources that will help students achieve the learning goals and complete the DT project. Here is an example of a learning plan for the second-grade City Plan project.

## Stage 3 — Learning Plan for the City Plan Project

**1.** Introduce the driving question and give a lesson on how to make observations and interview end users.

**2.** Visit and make observations of the local community and have students interview community members to gain empathy.

**3.** Provide instruction and model the process of synthesizing information gained from empathy work. As a class, develop a problem statement that includes the needs of the community members and insights learned from their interviews and observations.

**4.** Have students work in groups to brainstorm ideas that could help improve the community.

**5.** Have teams create a city plan that highlights their solutions to make the community better.

**6.** Plan the City Planning Expo where students present their city plans to demonstrate what they've learned to community members, peers, middle and high school students, and their families.

# Learning Management System: Seesaw and DT Digital Interactive Notebook

Seesaw is a great learning management system that my students and I use for our DT projects. It is supported on web browsers, iOS devices, and Android devices. This digital platform allows students to demonstrate their knowledge and skills through notes, photos, videos, drawings, and different files that can be imported from other apps like Google Drive. It provides each student with their own feed that captures their learning, growth, progress, and reflections.

It is also the ideal platform for the DT projects because every performance task from each phase can be completed and documented with one of its tools. Using Seesaw, students used the Note tool to post their findings from their empathy work and formulate their problem statement. They also brainstormed and sketched their ideas in the ideate phase using the Drawing tool, which allows them to create synchronized drawings, as well as record their voice explaining their ideas. Students who were more comfortable sketching their ideas on paper used the Photo tool to post their sketches onto their feed. Students also used the Photo tool to take pictures of their prototypes, showcasing the progression of the prototypes and the changes made for improvement. Finally, students documented their prototype tests by using the Video tool, enabling them to back and look at the footage to identify specific failure points. Seesaw also provides the commenting feature so that were able to reflect on what they learned.

Most importantly, Seesaw gives students the opportunity to be autonomous in their learning. They can independently jump to different phases and document their work at any given moment, depending on what was needed. For example, in the Schoolhouse project, students were able to prototype and test their schoolhouse designs whenever they were ready. When students finished their prototype, they did not have to ask me if they could test. Instead, they posted a picture of their prototype and then video recorded their testing session. After posting the video onto their feed, they added a comment that explained what occurred during the test, identified the failure points, and mentioned what improvements they planned to make for their next prototype. They then went back to the prototype phase to make their improvements and jumped right back to the testing phase; all of this was done independently with Seesaw.

If you and your students already use the G Suite, a platform of Google applications for educational work, at your school, then I recommend using my Design Thinking Digital Interactive Notebook (DTDIN). It is a Google Slides presentation that contains slides where students can document their work and learning and use the different DT tools that were discussed in chapters four to eight. You can find more information about this digital tool in the Appendix, on page 182.

# Conclusion

I would like to leave you with some advice when implementing DT into your classroom. First, start small. Form an after-school club where you have the flexibility to try a small-scale version of a DT project you've developed and learn what works, what doesn't work, and what would need to be improved. Many of the DT projects showcased in this book first started at an after-school club, where I rapid-prototyped my DT project ideas, worked out unexpected kinks, and acquired valuable insights that helped me to effectively implement the projects into my curriculum. It also provided me with the opportunity to try out new strategies in teaching and modeling specific DT principles and mindsets.

Second, understand that your DT projects will not be perfect. Don't put pressure on yourself to implement a flawless project where each DT phase contains high-quality learning activities and experiences for the students. Think of it as a low-res prototype which needs to go through multiple iterations. When developing a DT project, focus on one phase and mindset and try to implement/teach them really well. You can then add quality learning activities and experiences to the other DT phases of the project in the next iterations. For example, when first implementing the Schoolhouse Design project, I focused heavily on the prototype and test phases so that students would learn how to rapid prototypes, "build to think," and learn and improve from failures. It took us multiple iterations to get to this point. As I stated earlier in the book, our next iteration is to focus on the empathy phase, providing students with real end users to perform empathy work. A majority of the DT projects in this book contain phases that need to be improved in the next iteration.

Third, once you've implemented a DT project and feel ready to share it with others, capture your DT project through video. Use the footage you gain to create a movie that demonstrates the benefits of students using the DT process and engaging in DT mindsets to solve the real-world challenge of the project creatively. A movie is a great tool to gain buy-in from your grade level/department team, school, administrators, and parents.

The buy-in for DT in our school started with a movie I created of a project with Nalisha Keshaw's first-grade class. The movie illustrates how students utilized each phase of DT to define and solve their problem statement, and eventually, it was sent to the parents of Ms. Keshaw's students. Immediately, word got around among parents from other classes, who started to ask why their children were not learning DT in their classrooms. This sparked more teachers coming to me to develop or integrate DT projects. Eventually, DT was being used by every K–5 classroom. If you don't feel comfortable with creating a movie, I suggest creating a blog post that documents the journey of implementing your DT project and helps others gain an understanding of what DT is all about.

Lastly, use the DT method yourself to solve a problem or improve an experience that may exist in your classroom, school, or even in your personal life. It is one of the most powerful ways you can prepare yourself before implementing DT into your classroom. By going through the process, developing your DT mindsets, and conducting yourself in DT principles and behaviors, you will gain a deeper understanding of the method and better teach/model this creative problem-solving approach to your students.

When I was asked to start the KoLAB program, I decided to use the DT method to help me complete this immense project. By doing so, I was able empathize with the needs of the students, productively collaborate with multiple teachers and administrators, and creatively brainstorm, prototype, and test engaging, real-world curriculum. DT has helped me to develop a program that radically transformed the education we provide our students. It has helped us to optimistically develop structures that foster a culture of innovation, overcome unexpected obstacles, bring sustainability, and empower our teachers and students to become creative problem-solvers and behave like designers. Utilizing the method to develop this program has also helped me to gain a new level of consciousness, understanding, and appreciation for DT, which has helped me dramatically in teaching and modeling it my classroom.

Photo by Maggie Powers.

In 2016, Maggie Powers, a fellow Google Innovator, asked if I wanted to visit the d.school with her and her friends. To our surprise, her friend, Ellen Deutscher, arranged a sitting with David Kelley, the man behind IDEO and the d.school. After a short chat he was gracious enough to personally give us a tour of the d.school. We saw firsthand Stanford University students learning, brainstorming, and creating through the DT method. Kelley detailed how the d.school develops the creative potential of its students, provides them with project-based, student-centered learning experiences, and teaches them how to use DT to create positive change. For many, it is likely their first time being exposed to the human-centered method. I couldn't help but wonder, what if these students started learning about the process and mindsets at a younger age? What if they were exposed to it from their kindergarten year, all the way until high school? Imagine what students could potentially accomplish in the future. I encourage you to introduce your students to DT in your classrooms and empower them with the DT toolkit to become the positive, change agents that the future needs. Don't have them wait to learn DT later; give them a head start and equip them now.

# Appendix: Planning Materials and Resources

## Design Thinking Standards

Like I stated earlier, the development of the Design Thinking Standards (DTS) was heavily influenced by the work and teachings of the d.school and the K12 Lab Network. The structure of these standards replicates the structure of the Next Generation Science Standards. The standards (or performance expectations) are actionable and assessable learning goals that describe what students should be able to do when using the design thinking process.

These standards comprise design practices (skills that students will be able to do), core design ideas (knowledge that students will understand), and design mindsets (set of attitudes essential for effective application of design thinking). The following shows the empathize phase's performance expectations (ES) and the practices, core ideas, and the mindsets that the performance expectations consist of. You can find the complete set of standards at https://bit.ly/2q9n16D.

### Empathize Phase

#### Performance Expectations

Students who demonstrate understanding of the empathize phase can:

DTS-ES-1: Observe the behaviors, feelings, and patterns of the user in the context of their lives and design challenge.

DTS-ES-2: Engage with users and/or experts through conversations and interviews that incorporate open-ended questions to dig deeper for stories, feelings, emotion, and what is important to the user.

## Practices

Students will be able to ...

- Observe and engage with users, and immerse in the user experience.

- Identify the needs and insights of the users.

## Core Ideas

Students will understand that ...

- Empathy brings understanding of people, their physical and emotional needs and wants, the things that they do in their lives, and the context of the design challenge.

- Engagement with users through interaction and interviews exposes insights that can be utilized to create a more innovative solution.

- A beginner's mindset maintains an attitude of openness and puts aside biases that can restrict a person's ability to empathize.

## Mindsets Practiced

Design Thinking Mindsets

Students will demonstrate a set of attitudes that will help them ...

- Human centered

- Gain inspiration and direction from users and respond to human needs by placing the user at the center of all empathy work.

### Mindful of Process

Be thoughtful and reflective of the work being done, how the work is being done, and how the work will improve.

### Radical Collaboration

Collaborate and create partnerships with people of different disciplines as well as the users to develop innovative ideas and solutions.

# Digital Interactive Notebook

Interactive notebooks (IN) are tools that helps students document their learning. With traditional INs, students create charts, drawings, and write notes onto handouts, which they cut out and glue into their notebooks. Digital versions of these interactive notebooks enhance student learning by providing students the opportunity to create and explore ideas through the use of digital technologies.

I created a Design Thinking Digital Interactive Notebook (DTDIN) using Google Slides to help my students document and organize their work as they go through the different phases of the DT process. Google Slides is a presentation tool that allows students to access, create, and edit their work from any device that contains a browser or its dedicated mobile app. Through this tool, students can document their interview/observation notes and fill out an empathy map during the empathize phase, create mind maps and take photos of their sketched ideas in the ideate phase, and capture video of their user testing their prototypes in the test phase. Since Google Slides allows multiple people to collaborate and work on the same presentation, end users, classmates, and teachers can provide comments and feedback in real time.

The DTDIN also includes a table of contents that contains hyperlinks to specific phases, a slide for your DT project's driving question, and slides for different DT activities like Story Share-and-Capture and the 30 Circle Exercise. You can find this resource at https://bit.ly/2EkvJnJ.

The DTDIN Google Slides presentation gives students the ability to work on their DT project anywhere and on any digital device.

# References

ABC Nightline. "The Deep Dive: One Company's Secret Weapon for Innovation," YouTube, February 9, 1999, https://www.youtube.com/watch?v=M66ZU2PCIcM.

The Act Project, "Defining the ACT Project," May 7, 2017.

Adams, Dallon, "The Best of Biomimicry," *Digital Trends*, January 28, 2017, https://www.digitaltrends.com/cool-tech/biomimicry-examples.

Aedo, Cristian, Jesko Hentschel, Martin Moreno, and Javier Luque, *From Occupations to Embedded Skills: A Cross-Country Comparison* (Washington, DC: World Bank, 2013), https://elibrary.worldbank.org/doi/abs/10.1596/1813-9450-6560.

Autor, David H., and Brendan Price, *The Changing Task Composition of the US Labor Market: An Update of Autor, Levy, and Murnane (2003)* (Cambridge, MA: Massachusetts Institute of Technology, 2013), https://economics.mit.edu/files/11600.

Barker, Eric, "How to Become an Expert at Anything, According to Experts," *Time,* August 23, 2016, time.com/4461455/how-to-become-expert-at-anything.

Brandt, Anthony, and David Eagleman, "Where Do New Ideas Come From?" *Smithsonian*, October 21, 2017, https://www.smithsonianmag.com/innovation/where-do-new-ideas-come-from-180965202/.

Brew, A., "Approaches to the Scholarship of Teaching and Learning," in *Transforming a University: The Scholarship of Teaching and Learning in*

*Practice*, edited by A. Brew and J. Sachs, 1–10. Sydney: Sydney University Press, 2007.

Brock, Annie, and Heather Hundley, *The Growth Mindset Coach: A Teachers Month-by-Month Handbook for Empowering Students to Achieve* (Berkeley, CA: Ulysses Press, 2016).

Brown, Tim, *Change by Design* (New York: HarperCollins, 2009).

Buck Institute for Education, "Driving Question Tubric 2.0," http://www.bie.org/object/document/driving_question_tubric.

Buck Institute for Education, "What Is Project Based Learning (PBL)?" www.bie.org/about/what_pbl, accessed May 1, 2018.

Burnett, Bill, "Design Thinking: Method, Not Magic," Stanford Center for Creative Development, YouTube, April 20, 2016, https://www.youtube.com/watch?v=vSuK2C89yjA&index=21&list=PLYyk4fLjI-wR-XbKGBSlzN5p3jvD5iNs5B.

Burnett, Bill, "Design Thinking: Training Yourself to Be More Creative," Stanford Center for Creative Development, YouTube, May 3, 2013, https://www.youtube.com/watch?v=34EuT2KH2Lw.

Burnett, Bill, "Design Thinking: Transforming Teams," Stanford Center for Professional Development, YouTube, February 9, 2012, https://www.youtube.com/watch?v=BqKRcbxq7ck&list=PLYyk4fLjIwR-XbKGB-SlzN5p3jvD5iNs5B&index=26.

CBS News, "How to Design Breakthrough Inventions." YouTube, January 6, 2013. https://www.youtube.com/watch?v=_9TIspgTbLM.

Chang, Kenneth, "Like Water Off a Beetle's Back," *New York Times*, June 27, 2006, https://www.nytimes.com/2006/06/27/science/27find.html?_r=1.

Chi, Tom, "Rapid Prototyping Google Glass," TED-Ed, YouTube, January 22, 2013, https://www.youtube.com/watch?v=d5_h1VuwD6g.

City of Philadelphia, "Home Water Use," https://www.phila.gov/water/educationoutreach/Documents/Homewateruse_IG5.pdf.

Cleff, Andy, "'Plussing'—Learning and Working in a Collaborative Environment," AWEBER *Engineering*, September 24, 2014, engineering.aweber.com/plussing-learning-and-working-in-a-collaborative-environment.

Collins, WA, editor, "Development During Middle Childhood: The Years from Six to Twelve," National Research Council (US) Panel to Review the Status of Basic Research on School-Age Children (Washington, DC: National Academies Press, 1984).

Cooper-Wright, Matt, "Design Research from Interview to Insight: Part Two, Synthesising Insight," Design Research Methods, September 12, 2015, https://medium.com/design-research-methods/design-research-from-interview-to-insight-f6957b37c698.

Dam, Rikke, and Teo Siang, "Define and Frame Your Design Challenge by Creating Your Point of View and Ask 'How Might We,'" Interaction Design Foundation, 2017, https://www.interaction-design.org/literature/article/define-and-frame-your-design-challenge-by-creating-your-point-of-view-and-ask-how-might-we.

Dam, Rikke, and Teo Siang, "Stage 2 in the Design Thinking Process," Interaction Design Foundation, https://www.interaction-design.org/literature/article/stage-2-in-the-design-thinking-process-define-the-problem-and-interpret-the-results.

Dalton, Jonathan, "Five Principles of Effective INsight Definition." IDSA, December 22, 2016, http://www.idsa.org/news/insights/five-principles-effective-insight-definition.

Dalton, Jonathan, "What Is Insight? The Five Principles of Insight Definition," *Thrive*, March 28, 2016, thrivethinking.com/2016/03/28/what-is-insight-definition.

Design Kit, "Interview," http://www.designkit.org/methods/2.

d.K12 Lab Network, "Liberatory Design: Your Toolkit to Design for Equality," https://static1.squarespace.com/static/57c6b79629687f-de090a0fdd/t/58c8319bb3db2b7f6a7a22f0/1489514961988/Liberatory+Design+Cards.pdf.

d.school, About, https://dschool.stanford.edu/about.

d.school, *d.K12 Lab Network,* https://docs.google.com/presenta-tion/d/1S-7fZojfgGs3M3T110vaXZFztRvjmMdkCjJ4UiIQ5i0/present?ueb=true&slide=id.g1f13b8acbf_0_459.

d.school, *Empathy Fieldguide,* https://dschool-old.stanford.edu/sandbox/groups/dtbcresources/wiki/d9797/attachments/3832e/FIELDGUIDE-July-2015-Short-Probe-Version.pdf?sessionID=0728e00ac7d9b793a36b506bb13fa300297db775.

d.school, *Experiment Mixtape: Advancing Your Solution via Prototyping,* https://static1.squarespace.com/static/57c6b79629687f-de090a0fdd/t/58993c33893fc0620169bfc3/1486437447863/experiment-mixtape-v8.pdf.

d.school, *Get Started with Design Thinking,* https://dschool.stanford.edu/resources/getting-started-with-design-thinking.

d.school, *Ideate Mixtape: Generating Unexpected Ideas via Reframing Your Challenge,* https://static1.squarespace.com/static/57c6b79629687f-de090a0fdd/t/58993c9e579fb316f50f3f37/1486437546147/ideate-mixtape-v8.pdf.

d.school, *An Introduction to Design Thinking: Process Guide*, https://
static1.squarespace.com/static/57c6b79629687fde090a0fdd/t/58ac891
ae4fcb50f1fb2f1ab/1487702304601/Facilitator%27s+Guide_
Design+Thinking.pdf.

d.school, "The K12 Lab Wiki: Design Thinking Principles, Process, and
Methods," June 9, 2016, https://dschool-old.stanford.edu/groups/k12/
wiki/51de2/Design_Thinking_Principles_Process_and_Methods.html.

d.school, "The K12 Lab Wiki: Empathy Map," https://dschool-old
.stanford.edu/groups/k12/wiki/3d994/empathy_map.html.

d.school, "The K12 Lab Wiki: Interview Techniques," https://dschool-
old.stanford.edu/groups/k12/wiki/682ef/Interview_Techniques.html.

d.school, "The K12 Lab Wiki: POV Statements," https://dschool-old
.stanford.edu/groups/k12/wiki/41a18/POV_.html.

d.school, "Method: Feedback Capture Grid," https://dschool-old
.stanford.edu/sandbox/groups/dstudio/wiki/2fced/attachments/
1ba97/Feedback-Capture-Grid-Method.pdf?sessionID=d07c198d92501
ebb3eee4ff3da193b387130fcbf.

d.school, "Method: Testing with Users," https://dschool-old.stanford
.edu/sandbox/groups/dstudio/wiki/2fced/attachments/2ad84/Testing-
with-Users-Method.pdf?sessionID=9575b216cfa531b0cf12c34d3fc6d
0413c2cd7db.

d.school, "Method: Story Share and Capture," https://dschool-old
.stanford.edu/sandbox/groups/dstudio/wiki/2fced/attachments/
43f65/Story-Share-and-Capture-Method.pdf?sessionID=a4c32167e58
dc598ac57b770de7cb0f4f838ac50.

d.school, "Programs: K12 Lab," https://dschool.stanford.edu/programs/
k12-lab-network.

d.school, *Understand Mixtape: Discovering Insights via Human Engagement*, http://dschool-old.stanford.edu/wp-content/uploads/2012/02/understand-mixtape-v8.pdf.

d.school, *The Virtual Crash Course Playbook*, https://static1.square space.com/static/57c6b79629687fde090a0fdd/t/5899326a86e6c0878 c6e63f1/1486434929824/crashcourseplaybookfinal3-1-120302015105-phpapp02.pdf.

Dunn, Jeff, "It's Been 20 Years since Apple Re-Hired Steve Jobs— Here's How Much It's Grown in That Time," *Business Insider*, December 21, 2016, www.businessinsider.com/apple-growth-since-steve-jobs-chart-2016-12.

Dweck, Carol S., *Mindset: The New Psychology of Success* (New York: Ballantine, 2016).

Edutopia, "Pixar's Randy Nelson on the Collaborative Age," YouTube, July 2, 2010, www.youtube.com/watch?v=QhXJe8ANws8&feature= youtu.be&t=55s.

Friedman, Elsa, "David Kelley on Creative Confidence, Building to Think, Defining Innovation, Multidisciplinary Teams, and So Much More," *Rethinked*, July 15, 2013, rethinked.org/?p=4452.

GE Heathcare, "Changing Experiences through Empathy—The Adventure Series," http://thisisdesignthinking.net/2014/12/changing-experiences-through-empathy-ge-healthcares-adventure-series, accessed May 15, 2018.

GE Healthcare, "From Terrifying to Terrific: The Creative Journey of the Adventure Series," September 20, 2012, http://newsroom.gehealth care.com/from-terrifying-to-terrific-creative-journey-of-the-adventure-series.

Gil, Christina, "Interactive Notebooks," Edutopia, August 30, 2016, https://www.edutopia.org/blog/interactive-notebooks-no-special-hardware-christina-lovdal-gil.

Gray, Dave, "Updated Empathy Map Canvas," Medium.com, https://medium.com/the-xplane-collection/updated-empathy-map-canvas-46df22df3c8a.

Greenleaf, William, *Monopoly on Wheels: Henry Ford and the Selden Automobile Patent* (Detroit, MI: Wayne State University Press, 2011).

Hallermann, Sara, and John Larmer, *PBL in the Elementary Grades: Step-by-Step Guidance, Tools and Tips for Standards-Focused K-5 Projects*, Buck Institute for Education, 2011, https://www.guao.org/sites/default/files/biblioteca/PBL%20In%20the%20elementary%20Grades%20ocr.pdf.

Healey, Mick, "Strategies for Developing an Active Research Curriculum," University of Gloucestershire, UK, https://commons.georgetown.edu/m/media/resources/MickHealeySlides.ppt.

The Henry Ford, "Swift and Company's Meat Packing House, Chicago, Illinois, 'Splitting Backbones and Final Inspection of Hogs,' 1910–1915," https://www.thehenryford.org/collections-and-research/digital-collections/artifact/354536.

Home Hearts, "Skill Subjects vs. Content Subjects (The Key to Simplifying)," https://diyhomeschooler.com/2017/02/28/skill-subjects-vs-content-subjects-the-key-to-simplifying.

IDEO, About Ideo, https://www.ideo.com/about, accessed April 18, 2018.

IDEO, "A High-Tech Kidney Delivery System," January 2003, https://www.ideo.com/case-study/high-tech-kidney-delivery-system.

IDEO, "Design Thinking Thoughts by Tim Brown," https:// designthinking.ideo.com/?page_id=1542, accessed May 15, 2018.

IDEO, "Learn from Failure," 2015, https://vimeo.com/103471334.

IDEO, "A New Way to Vote for the People of Los Angeles," August 2015, https://www.ideo.com/case-study/a-new-way-to-vote-for-the-people-of-los-angeles.

IDEO slide presentation, "IDEO: Design Thinking Workshop 2016," Slide 22.

Interaction Design Foundation, "How Might We," https://public-media .interaction-design.org/pdf/How-Might-We.pdf.

Isaacs, Eric, "Forget about the Mythical Lone Inventor in the Garage," *Slate*, May 18, 2012, http://www.slate.com/articles/technology/future_ tense/2012/05/argonne_national_lab_director_on_the_myth_of_the_ lone_inventor_in_the_garage.html.

Jobs, Steve. "Text of Steve Jobs' Commencement Address (2005)," *Stanford News*, June 14, 2005, news.stanford.edu/2005/06/14/ jobs-061505.

Kelley, Tom, and David Kelley, "Three Creativity Challenges from IDEO's Leaders," *Harvard Business Review*, November 8, 2013, https:// hbr.org/2013/11/three-creativity-challenges-from-ideos-leaders.

Kelley, Tom, and David Kelley, *Creative Confidence: Unleashing the Creative Potential within Us All* (New York: Crown Business, 2013).

Kleon, Austin, *Steal Like an Artist: 10 Things Nobody Told You about Being Creative* (New York: Workman Publishing Company, 2012).

Lee, David, *Design Thinking: Digital Interactive Notebook,* (Yongin, Gyeonggi: EdTech, 2018).

Leung, Horace, "Air Jordan XVI Commercial, YouTube, September 11, 2014, https://www.youtube.com/watch?v=ijWObwahwvw.

Madson, Patricia Ryan, *Improv Wisdom: Don't Prepare, Just Show Up* (New York: Bell Tower, 2005).

McTighe, Jay, "What Is a Performance Task? (Part 1)." *Defined Learning*, April 10, 2015, blog.performancetask.com/what-is-a-performance-task-part-1-9fa0d99ead3b.

McTighe, Jay, and Grant Wiggins, "Understanding by Design Framework," www.ascd.org/ASCD/pdf/siteASCD/publications/UbD_WhitePaper0312.pdf.

Merchant, Brian, "The Secret Origin Story of the iPhone," *The Verge*, June 13, 2017, www.theverge.com/2017/6/13/15782200/one-device-secret-history-iphone-brian-merchant-book-excerpt.

MIT Mechanical Engineering, "An Iconic MIT Engineering Class," YouTube, March 11, 2014, https://www.youtube.com/watch?v=gXTcY0lO-pg.

MIT Mechanical Engineering, "A Tribute to David." YouTube, December 9, 2015, https://www.youtube.com/watch?v=i7qL2SN4LkE.

National Education Association, "Why Cultural Competence?" http://www.nea.org/home/39783.htm.

National Registrar of Historic Places, "Teaching Activities—Determining the Facts," https://www.nps.gov/nr/twhp/curriculumkit/lessons/edison/4facts1.htm.

Nesapiradana, Aldy Rizky, Rahmila Murtiana, and LBPP LIA Banjarmasin, "Improving Students' Fluency Through Voice Recording," http://www.academia.edu/5923355/Improving_students_fluency_through_voice_recording.

Next Generation Science Standards (NGSS), "Topic Arrangements of the Next Generation Science Standards," https://www.nextgenscience .org/sites/default/files/AllTopic.pdf.

Orr, Michael Curno, "Low-Resolution Prototyping: Ideation Tool and Implementation of Structured Methodology," *Texas ScholarWorks*, May 1, 2015, repositories.lib.utexas.edu/handle/2152/31991.

The Pearson Foundation and The Mobile Learning Institute, "Project-Based Learning at High-Tech High," Association for Learning Environments, YouTube, October 18, 2009, https://www.youtube.com/ watch?v=6rv_rmJYorE.

Roth, Bernard, *The Achievement Habit: Stop Wishing, Start Doing, and Take Command of Your Life* (New York: HarperCollins Publishing, 2015).

Satell, Greg, "It's Time to Bury the Idea of the Lone Genius Innovator," *Harvard Business Review*, April 8, 2016, hbr.org/2016/04/ its-time-to-bury-the-idea-of-the-lone-genius-innovator.

Seligman, Martin E. P., *Learned Optimism: How to Change Mind and Your Life* (New York: Vintage Books, 2006).

Stanford University, William Burnett Bio, 2017–2018, https:// explorecourses.stanford.edu/instructor/wburnett.

Stinson, Elizabeth, "IBMs Got a Plan to Bring Design Thinking to Big Business," *Wired*, June 3, 2017, www.wired.com/2016/01/ ibms-got-a-plan-to-bring-design-thinking-to-big-business.

Sugar, Rachel, and Richard Feloni, "29 Famous People Who Failed before They Succeeded," *Business Insider*, July 9, 2015, http://www .businessinsider.com/successful-people-who-failed-at-first-2015-7# walt-disney-was-fired-from-the-kansas-city-star-because-his-editor- felt-he-lacked-imagination-and-had-no-good-ideas-1.

Tesla, Nikola, as told to Alfred Albelli, "Radio Power Will Revolutionize the World," https://teslauniverse.com/nikola-tesla/articles/radio-power-will-revolutionize-world.

Tjendra, Jeffrey, "The Origins of Design Thinking," *Wired*, August 7, 2015, www.wired.com/insights/2014/04/origins-design-thinking.

Tofel, Kevin C., "BlackBerry: The One Time Smartphone Leader, Its Fall, and the Comeback that Never Happened," GigaOm, October 1, 2013, https://gigaom.com/2013/10/01/blackberry-the-one-time-smart-phone-leader-its-fall-and-the-comeback-that-never-happened.

Vasquez, Jo Anne, Cary Sneider, and Michael Comer, *STEM Lesson Essentials, Grades 3-8: Integrating Science, Technology, Engineering, and Mathematics* (Portsmouth, NH: Heinemann, 2013).

Vox, "How to Solve Problems Like a Designer." YouTube, September 21, 2017. https://www.youtube.com/watch?v=wOrmr5kT-48.

Wagner, Tony, *The Global Achievement Gap: Why Even Our Best Schools Don't Teach the New Survival Skills Our Children Need—and What We Can Do about It* (New York: Basic Books, 2010).

Wallace, David, "Course Description," Massachusetts Institute of Technology, web.mit.edu/2.009/www/courseinfo/CourseDescription .html.

Wikipedia, "Google Glass," April, 9 2018, en.wikipedia.org/wiki/ Google_Glass.

Wikipedia, "Peter Drucker," April 13, 2018, https://en.wikipedia.org/ wiki/Peter_Drucker.

Williams, Luke, *Disrupt: Think the Unthinkable to Spark Transformation in Your Business* (Upper Saddle River, NJ: Financial Times/Prentice Hall, 2011).

Wilson, Donna, and Marcus Conyers, *Teaching Students to Drive Their Brains: Metacognitive Strategies, Activities, and Lesson Ideas* (Alexandria, VA: ASCD, 2016).

X Company, Home Page, https://x.company/, accessed May 15, 2018.

Yang, YuHsiu, and Melissa Huang, *Design & Thinking—a Documentary on Design Thinking*, designthinkingmovie.com/.

Yokohama International School, #BeyondLaptops, http://blogs.yis.ac.jp/beyondlaptops/about.

Yoo, Youngjin, and Kyungmook Kim, "How Samsung Became a Design Powerhouse," *Harvard Business Review*, August 10, 2015, https://hbr.org/2015/09/how-samsung-became-a-design-powerhouse.

# Index

# Acknowledgments

First and foremost, I would like to state that everything that was included in this book would not have been possible without the inspirational DT work of IDEO, K12 Lab Network, and the d.school. Their open educational resources inspired me to use DT to bring transformational change to my school and empower my students through the implementation of DT into the classroom. I would also like to thank the specific individuals from these amazing organizations from whom I've learned greatly through their work: David Kelley, Tim Brown, and David Clifford.

For the book itself, I would like to thank Bridget Thoreson for approaching me to write this book and facilitating the whole process from the beginning to the end, and the editors at Ulysses Press, Shayna Keyles and Renee Rutledge, who skillfully helped edit and craft my book to what it is today. In addition, I am so grateful for the following people who were kind enough to take their time to review my drafts, share their expertise, and provide valuable feedback that greatly improved my book: Graham Willard, Sarah Marslender, David Clifford, Stacy Stephens, and Angela Spitzman.

Many of the DT projects in the book could not have happened without the collaboration of numerous teachers and administrators. I would like to thank the following people for taking the time to develop meaningful projects for our students:

- Co-Design Teachers: Becca Goess and Heidi Peterson

- Science Specialists: Elizabeth DiRenzo, Gene MacLachlan, and Jeremy Jacobsen

- Administrators: Danielle Rich, Travis Peterson, and Tara Verenna

- Kindergarten teachers: Paul Duffy and Jessica Jacobsen

- First-grade teachers: Helen Nam, Erna Lemmon, Amy Cabaluna, Katie Thomas

- Second-grade teachers: Denise Brohm, Alice Ahn, Virginia Nakauchi, Leann Norton, and Thomas Cabaluna

- Third-grade teachers: Jon Barry, Sally Merriman, Sarah Donaldson, and Katie Fleetwood

- Fourth-grade teachers: Angela Spitzman, Molly Ball, Colleen McCabe, and Shikha Kuckreja

- Fifth-grade teachers: Jay Keshaw, Stephanie Cory, David Archer, and Erin Curtiss

- Specialists: Megan Godek, Megan Greene, Karen Luu, Diana Caudill, Chaoran Yao, and Marsha Bycraft

I cannot forget to give a shout out to my wonderful students who amaze me every day with their kindness, intelligence, enthusiasm, and optimism. Most importantly, I'd like to thank my wife, Angela, and my son for motivating me to do my best in everything I do.

# About the Author

**David Lee** was the coordinator of the K–5 KoLAB Program at Korea International School. He taught Design to K–5 students with his coteacher, Heidi Peterson. They taught and modeled the design thinking process and its mindsets so that students can apply what they've learned in different subject areas to projects where they develop innovative solutions to solve complex problems. David currently teaches at the Singapore American School in Singapore.